Moving on in Your Career

In today's competitive market a higher degree will not necessarily lead to a career in higher education. Researchers need to know how to enhance their career prospects and how to look further into the wide range of career options open to them elsewhere.

Moving on in Your Career shows researchers what is required to make a continuing career in academic research or lecturing and gives advice on taking alternative career paths. **Barbara Graham** and **Lynda Ali** draw on their experience of careers guidance in higher education to outline various options in which researchers can use the skills developed at university. They advise on sources of advertised and unadvertised vacancies and how to use methods such as speculative applications and the internet. *Moving on in Your Career* also provides practical exercises and ideas to enhance essential job-search and self-presentation skills.

With its special focus on the skills acquired through academic research and how to use them to pursue a wide variety of career options *Moving on in Your Career* will appeal to postgraduate students and researchers as well as research managers, careers advisers and all who have responsibility for students and researchers.

Lynda Ali is a senior careers adviser at Edinburgh University and trains careers advisers in counselling skills. **Barbara Graham** is Director of Strathclyde University Careers Service and a member of national committees on career issues for contract researchers. Their previous publications include *The Counselling Approach to Careers Guidance*, Routledge 1996.

Moving on in Your Career

A guide for academic researchers
and postgraduates

Lynda Ali
and
Barbara Graham

London and New York

First published 2000 by RoutledgeFalmer
11 New Fetter Lane, London, EC4P 4EE

Simultaneously published in the USA and Canada
by RoutledgeFalmer
29 West 35th Street, New York, NY 10001

RoutledgeFalmer is an imprint of the Taylor & Francis Group

@ 2000 Lynda Ali and Barbara Graham

Typeset in Goudy by
Curran Publishing Services Ltd
Printed and bound in Great Britain by
Biddles Ltd, Guildford and King's Lynn

British Library Cataloguing in Publication Data
A catalogue record for this book is available
from the British Library

Library of Congress Cataloging in Publication Data
Ali, Lynda, 1946–
   Moving on in your career : a guide for academicresearchers and
   postgraduates
   / Lynda Ali and Barbara Graham.
   200 p. 15.6 x 23.4 cm.
   Includes bibliographical references and index.
   1. College teaching – Vocational guidance – Great Britain. 2. College
   graduates – Employment – Great Britain. 3. Career changes – Great
   Britain. 4. Job hunting – Great Britain.
   I. Graham, Barbara, 1947 Aug 3–
   II Title.
   LB1778.4.G7A45   2000
   378.1'2'02341–dc21   99-44350
                                                                CIP

ISBN 0-415-17869-X (hard: alk. paper)
ISBN 0-415-17870-3 (pbk.: alk. paper)

Contents

Exercises

Figures

Tables

Acknowledgements

Many people have contributed to the making of this book. It was inspired by the writings of Dr Margaret Newhouse of the Office of Career Services at Harvard University. The many contract research staff with whom the authors have worked contributed to our understanding of the needs of the potential audience and the kinds of advice which they found to be helpful.

Thanks are due to Mr Gordon Anderson of the Scottish Higher Education Funding Council who supplied statistics for chapter 1. We are also indebted to the people who let us use their stories for the case studies.

Without the encouragement of Helen Fairlie, our editor, and the patience and perseverance of Andrea Gibson, who typed the text, the book would not have seen the light of day. We are grateful for their support.

Lynda Ali
Barbara Graham

Foreword

As we approach the twenty-first century, the rate of change in society, in technology, in all our affairs, is remarkable. The *Economist* captured the necessity for universities to adapt to this volatile, competitive environment when it wrote in its 20 June 1992 edition:

> The universities are destined to change more in the next five years than they have done in the previous half-century . . . This pell-mell expansion will soon require the universities to rethink everything from how they teach to where they get their income.

It is therefore essential that all universities, large and small, old or new, research-led or training and teaching-led, have a strategic planning process in place where the emphasis is clearly on innovation and creativity and staff development.

Left to themselves, however, organisations would change very little, because their members have two over-riding needs: for stability and security. Many members of staff have traditionally placed a lot of energy into keeping things as they are, a dynamic conservatism if you will. In academe, in former years, such people would rush to the barricades to defend hallowed traditions and ideas. Indeed their notion of a satisfactory future was a return to the idealised past. How times have changed!

Due to the rapid and spectacular advances in communications and information technologies we are moving towards what some have called the 'Information Society', but which is better termed the 'Knowledge Society'. In this environment, success will depend crucially on the ability of individuals to be adaptable, to learn new skills and to make sense of an abundant quantity of information. Knowledge is information put to work; it is about understanding: it is what enables people to make judgements, interpret events, solve problems and create new products and services.

In an academic environment there can be widespread resentment of corporate approaches to university management and to central oversight of academic activities. Selectivity can appear quite confrontational to cherished academic icons of collegiality and the notion that all academics should be treated equally.

Therefore, as in any competitive business, there is a need to engage staff at all levels in strategic thinking where the premium is on imagination. It is also important that university vice-chancellors and principals adopt two guiding principles advocated by Thomas Jefferson and Winston Churchill, respectively. The former advised that:

No more good must be attempted than the people can bear,

while Churchill remarked that:

The art of progress is to preserve order amid change and to preserve change amid order.

Developments in teaching, research and the organisation and funding of universities have placed an increased emphasis on continuing professional development as a significant ingredient of effective change management. Not before time, funding councils and professional institutions are introducing various initiatives to help influence management practice in higher education. Particular attention is being placed on the important category of staff who are employed on short-term contacts with little prospect of permanent full-time academic employment. It is vital that this cohort, while developing highly specialised research skills, also acquires a broader range of competencies which will stand them in good stead when they leave academe. Their time at the university needs to be viewed as a preparation for a lifetime of self-education.

This new book on how academic researchers can move on in their career is very timely and will be welcomed by all those who are involved in higher education. Its authors Barbara Graham and Lynda Ali have extensive experience of careers guidance including work with postgraduates and contract research staff. They therefore fully understand the issues involved and have empathy with the target audience for this book. Barbara has served with distinction on the national Research Careers Initiative which I chair.

The book gives equally helpful advice to readers seeking advancement in their academic careers and to those wishing to change their career direction. Most of the case studies are based on real people with whom the authors have worked. They are to be commended on producing a book which is both informative and very readable. The advice it contains will have powerful implications for staff in universities who wish to fulfil their real potential.

Professor Sir Gareth Roberts
Vice-Chancellor, University of Sheffield
Chair, Research Careers Initiative

Introduction

This book arose from concern expressed in the UK and the USA about the large numbers of highly qualified scholars seeking a small number of academic research and teaching posts in higher education. Depending on academic mentors for advice and expecting their academic record to speak for itself, many scholars have never sought professional careers advice to explore the full range of career options open to them. Many also have little knowledge of the job-seeking skills necessary to improve their prospects of gaining either an academic post or a job in an alternative field.

The book aims to help readers who are trying to decide between a career in academic research and teaching or an alternative occupation which will use their research-related skills. People at various stages may find it useful: undergraduates contemplating a career in research; postgraduate students preparing to seek employment after graduation; contract research staff and teaching assistants who are finding difficulty in securing permanent posts in higher education; and established academics who, for whatever reasons, are seeking a change of career direction.

Previous writing on this subject is based on the American experience, which does not always translate well into the UK context. The advice in this book relates to the UK labour market. It is based on the authors' experience of working on career issues and job search strategies with research students, contract research staff and other members of academic staff in higher education.

The authors make no value judgements on whether an academic or a non-academic career is the 'better' option; this can be decided only by the individual in the light of personal preferences and circumstances. For some people, it may be possible to combine elements of both types of work in a 'portfolio career'. The job search strategies and self-presentation skills described in the book can be applied to either context.

How to use this book

All that you have to bring to *Moving on in Your Career* is an open mind and a willingness to explore new insights, which are the basis of all good research. This book is designed to be used in two ways. It can be read straight through if you wish to gain an insight into the employment situation in universities, examine some alternative career options and follow a logical process of how to move from career choice to securing a post. Alternatively, it can be used as a reference manual as you move through the various stages of the career planning process, which may take months or even years to achieve. In the first instance it may be helpful to read through the book to gain an overview of its contents, which are outlined below.

Part I: focus on higher education

Part I provides the context in which academic researchers are choosing whether to follow an academic career or to seek to use the skills and experience gained through academic research in a different setting. In this first chapter of the book there is an explanation of how and why the staffing structure of universities and colleges of higher education has changed. The authors review national initiatives designed to ensure that well-qualified graduates should achieve satisfying career development, either within or beyond higher education, and should then be able to contribute to the national economy in a wide variety of settings. The chapter also outlines the advantages and disadvantages inherent in this situation for people starting out on an academic career.

Part II: focus on yourself

Part II has a different focus. It invites you to be proactive in thinking about your skills, interests, values and preferences. The text gives you a framework for career planning, and acts as a prompt to individual reflection which will help you to clarify what you want from your career and what you have to offer employers.

Chapter 2 gives an overview of the stages involved in developing a career plan and helps you to understand the process by which people make career choices. Internal and external influences which affect both your potential and the opportunities available to you are examined.

Chapter 3 looks more closely at self-assessment, which is the foundation for all sound career planning. Exercises in the text help you to gather evidence of your skills, interests, values, personality and present circumstances which you can use not only in career choice, but also when presenting yourself via applications and interviews.

In chapter 4 you will discover how to use key skills and interests commonly shared by academic researchers as a focal starting point in a range of techniques designed to generate career options for consideration. These techniques include simple brainstorming, workbooks and computer-aided guidance systems.

Information on careers is the subject of chapter 5. After considering what types of information are needed in order to make decisions about careers, the chapter provides advice on potential sources of information, including careers services, professional bodies, practitioners and the Internet. The chapter closes with advice on how to avoid information overload.

Chapter 6 offers a framework for decision-making on careers, using the structured material gathered in previous chapters. The stages in this process will help you to weigh up the cost and consequences of each option before you decide to pursue it.

Part III: focus on career options

The concept of what constitutes a career has undergone radical change in recent years. While some people may spend their working years in a single profession, few retain an expectation of being in one job for life. Many people will change their occupation: perhaps moving from a practitioner to a management role on promotion, or changing direction after re-training in a different field, either voluntarily or following redundancy.

In this context, it is important not to confine yourself to too narrow a range of career options when considering your future direction. Part III of the book introduces some possibilities.

Chapter 7 looks at some classic routes into academic careers and highlights some of the essential knowledge and experience which you should gain if you wish to progress in this direction. Case studies demonstrate how this has worked for three academics.

In chapter 8 further case studies show how academic researchers have successfully diversified into a very wide range of occupations; some close to, but others far removed from their degree discipline. This chapter closes by inviting you to reflect on messages from these graduates and to contemplate their significance for you.

Part IV: focus on getting a job

Following a decision on career choice – be that an academic or an alternative route – you need to persuade an employer to give you a job. In a highly competitive world this means that every aspect of your job search and self presentation needs to be highly professional.

In chapter 9 advice is given on sources of vacancies for academic and other posts. This includes access to the 'hidden job market' of unadvertised vacancies, which accounts for up to 60 per cent of vacancies. There is also advice on how to use the Internet for your job search.

Chapters 10 to 12 concentrate on how to convince selectors that you are the best candidate for either an academic or a non-academic post. Advice is given on how to write effective CVs, targeted at higher education and other sectors. A chapter on applications helps you to understand why employers ask certain questions, and how you can tackle them. Hints on successful interviews include sample questions which might arise at interviews in higher education and elsewhere.

Chapter 13 deals with job search strategy and alerts you to common pitfalls often encountered by job seekers. You are invited to review the main messages of the book and to commit yourself to further action by completing a chart of actions which you will take within a specified timescale in order to achieve your career objective.

Working through the book systematically will help you to take a logical approach to thinking about what you want from your career and how you can achieve it. Focusing your thinking on these issues is the first essential step towards gaining entry to a field of employment which will give you continuing satisfaction and the sense of personal fulfilment which comes from knowing that you are using your talents in a context which suits your temperament, skills and values.

Part I

Focus on higher education

Chapter I

Understanding the context
Academic staff in higher education

Since the middle of the 1980s there has been a sharp increase not only in the student population of UK universities, but also in academic staff numbers. It is the way in which staff numbers have increased, however, that has changed the outlook for people proposing to pursue a career in higher education.

The major expansion has been in the category of academic research staff and lecturers employed on short term contracts, while the number of academic staff on permanent contracts has remained almost static. In the period 1977/78 to 1995/96, contract research staff numbers increased by almost 500 per cent, while the equivalent increase for permanent academic staff was around 2 per cent.[1] Figures for 1997/98 show that 28 per cent of all academic staff in UK higher education were contract research staff.[2] If the trend continues at the same pace, it is likely that by the end of the century around one-third of academics may be in this category.

This skewed distribution of the rate of increase among temporary and permanent staff is largely due to the way in which institutions are funded, particularly for their research activities. A high proportion of research funding comes in the form of block grants to cover projects lasting from a few months to between three and five years. Allocations from the various national funding councils are given on an ongoing basis, but during the middle and late 1990s the cost efficiencies required by the funding councils have meant an effective reduction of funding council grants in real money terms.

In the 1990s government funding policies for higher education introduced another volatile element into the financial planning scenario for universities. The Research Assessment Exercise, which is conducted every four years, and the quality assurance audits, which review academic departments' teaching provision on a regular cycle, introduced financial incentives and penalties depending on institutions' performance.

The uncertainty of the outcome of these assessments makes it very difficult for institutions to commit themselves to permanent contracts with all staff. Even the most careful strategic planning for the submission of records of research can come adrift if the basis on which funding is allocated alters from one year to the next, leaving institutions with unexpected shortfalls in research-related income.

Against this background of 'payment by results', institutions cannot afford to carry any non-productive staff. In the wake of the Research Assessment Exercises of the late 1990s some institutions chose to channel their research funding towards their most able researchers while firmly directing other staff towards teaching and administrative duties. In the case of institutions with severe financial difficulties this realignment policy was carried even further by inviting eligible staff who were less active in research to take early retirement or voluntary – or even compulsory – redundancy.

It is clear that at the end of the twentieth century institutions of higher education are in a state of great flux. The rate of expansion in the last decade of the century has changed higher education in ways which a pre-Robbins observer would never have thought possible. As in all situations of great change, this poses both opportunities and threats for those wishing to set out on an academic career.

The purpose of this chapter is to explain the current structure of academic staffing and the most common route into an academic post via a temporary post. It also includes a summary of the advantages and disadvantages of temporary appointments for entrants to an academic career in higher education.

The composition of academic staff in higher education

Given the strong competition for academic posts, it is unlikely that a graduate with a recently completed Ph.D. or first degree will step directly into a permanent teaching or research post. Typical advertisements for lecturing posts ask for candidates who have 'proven teaching ability' and who are 'active and publishing researchers'. Even where such requirements are not specifically spelled out, competition from well-qualified candidates can be so great that such experience effectively becomes a prerequisite. Thus, the aspiring academic is often obliged to gain employment in the first instance via a tutorial assistantship or a short-term contract research post.

The likelihood of new entrants being channelled via this route is emphasised by figures on the distribution of academic staff in UK universities. The tables in this chapter analyse the staffing distribution in terms of subject area, staffing grades, age and gender.

Subject area

From the figures in Table 1.1 it is possible to conclude that entry to an academic route is more likely to occur via a short-term contract in sciences and engineering than in other disciplines, as between one-third and a half of all staff working in these fields are on fixed-term contracts. There is a limit, however, to the inferences which can be drawn from these statistics. For instance, the figures do not indicate the level of competition for entry into certain fields. If, for example, there are many Ph.D. chemists vying for a relatively large number of research posts, the competition there may be much more intense than it is for a small

Table 1.1 Distribution of academic staff by subject area, 1997–98

Discipline	Total	Contract research as % of total staff
Medicine, dentistry	31,457	37
Biological, physical & general sciences	19,624	50
Agricultural, forestry & veterinary science	2,681	33
Engineering, technology	13,903	39
Architecture, planning	2,695	13
Maths, computing science	8,034	21
Business and management studies, catering and hospitality management	9,085	9
Social studies	12,294	17
Languages, humanities	11,098	8
Design and creative arts	6,676	4
Education	6,580	8
University administrative, academic & and central services	960	21
Total	125,087	28

Source: Extracts from a table produced by the Scottish Higher Education Funding Council, based on Higher Education Statistics Agency figures on staffing in UK higher education.

number of research posts in Information Science, if relatively fewer qualified people in that discipline opt for an academic research career.

Staffing grades

An analysis in Table 1.2 of the grades in which temporary and permanent staff were distributed in 1997/98 shows that while there is a reasonable prospect of progression from the lecturer to the senior lecturer grade, the distribution of researchers is much more heavily skewed towards the lower end of the scale, with 84 per cent of researchers in graded posts on grade 1. This clustering towards the lower end of the salary scales is probably higher than these figures suggest, as the category 'researcher, other' includes many staff on pay rates which, although different, are not better than grade 1 rates.

Length of contract

The realisation that most academic researchers are on short term contracts raises the question, 'How temporary is temporary?'. This is a difficult question to answer as it is common for short extensions on contracts to be given, either in order to complete a piece of research or as a bridging mechanism, in an effort to keep a good researcher in the hope that additional funding will enable further research to be undertaken.

No reliable national figures are available, but a pilot study of over 500

Table 1.2 Distribution of academic staff by staffing grade, 1997–98

Grade	Number	Contract researchers as % of total staff
Researcher, grade 1	23,628	95
Researcher, grade 2	3,519	84
Researcher, grade 3	770	77
Researcher, grade 4	121	64
Researcher, other[a]	5,733	86
Lecturer	49,459	3
Senior lecturer	19,986	1
Professor/head	9,672	1
Other grades[a]	12,199	15
All grades[b]	125,087	28

Source: Extracts from SHEFC/HESA statistics — as for Table 1.1

Notes
a A high proportion of staff on 'other' grades are at the lower end of the salary scale.
b Figures cover staff working in a teaching, research or teaching and research capacity for at least 25% of full-time for the session.

researchers in Scotland showed that the average length of contract in 1997 was two and a half years.[3] This is probably slightly longer than the national average as medical and related researchers were over-represented in this sample and they are known from this study to have longer contracts than researchers in other disciplines. The length of contracts for the whole group ranged from one month to five years.

In this cohort over 30 per cent were on their first contract, while nearly 20 per cent had had five or more contracts. The high proportion in the early stages of a research career is consistent with the rapid expansion of contract research in recent years. At the same time, this large influx also creates a difficulty for the deployment of these staff in a profession which currently holds little prospect for advancement. If there is little prospect of promotion, or even of securing a long-term post near the bottom of the career ladder in research, then the only viable alternative is to encourage a substantial outflow from research into other academic or non-academic posts.

Age

Table 1.3 shows that while contract research staff in 1997/98 were predominantly under forty, most other academic staff were over forty, with a substantial proportion being fifty and older. To some extent that is a healthy pattern of distribution, suggesting that over the next two decades there will be a steady mass exodus of staff from lecturing posts as older staff reach normal retirement age or take advantage of early retirement schemes. This displacement should create vacancies for academics who have been in temporary lecturing or research posts. In current financial circumstances, however, a curb may be placed on this flow into permanent jobs, as institutions either are unable to replace staff, or

Table 1.3 Distribution of academic staff by age group, 1997–98

Age	Contract research %*	Permanent research %	Other academic %
Under 30	39	14	5
30–39	43	34	26
40–49	12	27	34
50 and over	5	25	35

Source: Extracts from SHEFC/HESA statistics – as for Table 1.1

Note
* Percentages are of total for each category of staff.

move an even higher proportion of their staff on to short term contracts in order to retain flexibility of financial planning.

Gender

As with age groups, there is an uneven distribution of academic staff by gender. Table 1.4 shows that women have better representation among contract research staff than they do among other academic groups. Although representation of women in the latter is slowly improving, as in most professions, there is a concentration of women in the lower grades of staff.

Staff development initiatives

From the mid-1990s onwards an impetus for improvement in conditions of employment and career development prospects has come from three directions:

Table 1.4 Staffing grades of female academics, 1997–98

| Grade | Proportion of women in each grade (%) | | |
	Contract research	Permanent research	Other academic
Researcher, grade 1	41	38	45
Researcher, grade 2	36	24	32
Researcher, grade 3	29	19	31
Researcher, grade 4	10	25	10
Researcher, other	39	39	45
Lecturer	35	34	38
Senior lecturer	22	25	21
Professor/head	13	21	9
Other grades	39	25	43
All grades	39	31	31

Source:- Extracts from SHEFC/HESA statistics, as for Table 1.1

- unions
- government
- funding bodies in alliance with higher education institutions.

Each of these three sectors has approached the issues from a different stand-point and with differing motivations. These initiatives are outlined below.

Unions

From the figures cited in Table 1.1, unions realised that their constituency was changing. They were increasingly representing – or had the potential to represent – a large number of transitory staff. Some of these had very brief contracts and were for the most part unwilling or unable to press for improved conditions, partly because of their uncertainty about being able to continue in an academic career, but also because of a lack of knowledge of how to do so and because of a reluctance to be labelled as militants lest that should spoil their long-term employment prospects. As temporary employees, many of these contract academics did not join a union, which in turn meant a decline in the proportion of higher education staff represented by unions. If allowed to continue, this could damage unions' negotiating powers.

Out of a sense of natural justice towards those of their members on short-term contracts, coupled with an understandable self-interest in wishing to represent the main growth sector in higher education staffing, the unions began to marshal facts on contract staff and to agitate on their behalf for better conditions and prospects of employment.

The Association of University Teachers (AUT) has been particularly active in this respect. As far back as 1991 the AUT produced a code of good practice on employment issues relating to contract researchers.[4] While helpful as a guideline to enlightened institutions, and to researchers themselves as an indication of how they might hope to be treated, this document, like all such codes, spelled out optional rather than mandatory practices. Nor did it have even the force of a 'gentlemen's agreement' as it had not been negotiated with representatives of employers.

In order to emphasise the urgency of dealing with unsatisfactory conditions experienced by many contract academics, the AUT bolstered its arguments by producing incontrovertible evidence of bad practice which was not conducive to good working relationships nor ultimately to high productivity by staff on fixed-term contracts. Instances of lack of sick pay, holiday and maternity leave entitlements, involvement in the corporate life of departments and any guidance with career development came to light in the research. This resulted in a 1994 report on the employment conditions of contract research staff, which received widespread publicity in higher-education circles.[5]

In order to press home the point that temporary staff should have entitlements, the AUT supported researchers who took their universities to tribunals on the issue of assistance in finding employment on the termination of a contract.

Although the efforts of unions did not result in a marked improvement in terms of employment for staff, they did succeed in placing the issue of contract research staff in particular higher on universities' agendas, at a time when funding constraints might otherwise have inclined them to overlook the needs of this group of staff.

Government

Government interest in the effective career management of academic staff stems from a desire to ensure that talented people in whose education the nation has invested should be enabled to make a significant contribution to the country's economy, not only within the higher education sector, but across other sectors. Concern about Britain's ability to compete effectively with other nations in a highly technological age means that the emphasis of the government's investigation into the employment of contract research staff has been centred on those qualified in science and technology rather than in other disciplines.

The title of a government White Paper in 1993 – *Realising Our Potential: a Strategy for Science, Engineering and Technology* – hinted at the philosophy behind the investigation, namely that developments which are good for the economy are likely to be good for individuals' career prospects, and vice versa.[6]

As a result of this report, a Select Committee of the House of Lords was established to look in greater depth at the issue of career patterns and prospects for academic scientists. This Select Committee examined evidence from universities, contract researchers, established academics and employers. It also examined the situation in America, where there is a serious over-supply of Ph.D. graduates seeking to enter academic research, and reported on initiatives to encourage highly qualified scientists to enter other occupations and to set up their own businesses in 'spin-out companies', based on their academic research.

Following its fact-finding mission, the Select Committee issued a report in 1995, which made specific recommendations to funding bodies and higher education institutions on how conditions and prospects for academic scientists might be improved.[7] Like the AUT code of practice, this document had no force of law, but emanating from Parliament, the report was used by the Government to give a directive to institutions and funding bodies to address in a serious manner the issues which had come to light.

Funding bodies and higher education institutions

The Concordat

In 1995 the Government specifically directed the research councils to work with higher education representatives to establish definite criteria for improved career management and development of contract research staff funded by the research councils. Discussions resulted in the following year in the signing of *A Concordat on Contract Research Staff Career Management*.[8] The signatories included the main research councils, the Royal Society, the British Academy and the three main bodies representing higher education institutions.[9]

Strictly speaking, some categories of contract staff were excluded from the Concordat, namely contract researchers funded by bodies other than the signatory research councils (for example, industrial sponsors and medical charities such as the Wellcome Foundation) and other categories of staff such as temporary lecturers and academic related staff. In practice, however, it would be difficult and not desirable for university personnel offices to differentiate between members of staff who are in the same category solely on the basis of how they are funded. In their efforts to implement the Concordat, institutions have therefore tended to adopt the same policies for all contract research staff, irrespective of their source of funding, although these arrangements have not necessarily been extended to other categories of temporary staff with similar needs.

The Concordat attempts to take a realistic view of the prospects of contract researchers. It starts from the assumption that

> an established career in academia or, exclusively, academic research, is realistic only for a minority.

The agreement requires institutions to put into place effective policies and practices for various improved conditions of employment for contract research staff, including:

> career guidance and development, for example to inform decisions by contract research staff on a change of career direction if the opportunities are limited or if they do not wish to remain in research or are not suited to such a career, and encouragement of talented researchers with advice on opportunities inside and outside the employing institution.

This set a significant precedent, for universities and colleges are not held to such a specific obligation to manage and develop the careers of any other category of staff. The agreement of the representatives of higher education institutions to acknowledge such an obligation towards temporary staff indicates their degree of concern about the routeing of talented academics into higher education and other sectors of employment.

The resources for achieving this major initiative were left somewhat vague in the Condordat, where it is simply stated that:

> the funding bodies will, with the universities, colleges and other interested parties, consider ways of strengthening the provision of career information and advice for contract research staff and fellows.

Despite the initial lack of clarity about the resource issues for the implementation of its requirements, the Concordat clearly implied that after a period of grace, the continued award of grants by funding bodies would depend upon assurances of institutions' compliance with the terms of the Concordat. A progress review was scheduled for eighteen months after the Concordat launch date of September 1996, with a subsequent review by all parties to the Concordat on a biennial basis. As an interim measure, the Committee of Vice-Chancellors and Principals required all institutions to submit by July 1997 'policy statements of the provisions for career development, management and conditions of employment which the Concordat asks to be given to each contract researcher.'[10]

To ensure progress, the signatories to the Concordat asked every institution to nominate an individual responsible for contract research staff, and set up the Research Careers Initiative Working Party to monitor implementation of the Concordat in respect of training, careers guidance and the future career structure for academic researchers. The working party's investigations and recommendations convinced the Office of Science and Technology that there was a need to invest resources in careers guidance for contract research staff, and funding was provided to develop materials tailored especially for this group.

Compliance with the Concordat was firmly on the agenda, but in the tradition of UK higher education, institutions were left with a large degree of latitude as to how and with what degree of vigour they fulfilled their new obligations. The next section of this chapter shows how two agencies set the pace in enabling institutions to adopt a practical, constructive approach to the challenges facing them.

Implementing the Concordat

THE SHEFC CONTRACT RESEARCH STAFF INITIATIVE

In parallel with the movement which resulted in the Concordat, and prompted at least in part by the AUT survey of contract research staff, the Scottish Higher Education Funding Council (SHEFC) launched its Contract Research Staff Initiative towards the end of 1995. One of the underlying objectives of this Initiative was to retain top quality researchers in Scotland and to attract others from elsewhere by demonstrating good practice in the employment and career development of contract research staff in Scottish higher education institutions. At the time of writing (1999) SHEFC is the only one of the national funding councils to have allocated funding for the improvement of conditions and career prospects for any category of temporary staff.

Following the appointment of an Initiative Co-ordinator, all Scottish higher education institutions designated a senior person to be responsible for liaison with SHEFC on contract research staff. In an attempt to involve institutions in ownership of the Initiative, SHEFC invited bids for projects which would fulfil a number of objectives outlined in the Initiative's manifesto. This resulted in individual universities and groups of institutions undertaking projects, including research skills training for contract research staff and management training courses for research managers.

On the career development front, a consortium of Scottish higher education careers services, the Scottish Graduate Careers Partnership, developed a variety of projects to produce materials and models of courses which individual institutions could subsequently use with their contract staff. These included:

- career development courses
- a resource pack and a training course for trainers
- a self-help careers manual for research
- a guide to job seeking via the Internet
- a conference on career options for researchers
- a pilot survey of the destinations of contract research staff.

A report on the Initiative and its impact is available from SHEFC's Research Funding and Policy Branch.[11]

The Prosper Wales Initiative

The Prosper Wales Initiative was launched by a partnership of the University of Wales, the Welsh Office and the Welsh Development Agency. Based at Cardiff and Swansea this programme's aims were to retain academic researchers within the Welsh economy and to encourage small and medium enterprises to recognise the value of employing highly skilled workers in order to develop their businesses. In addition to running career development courses for contract researchers, Prosper Wales produced portfolios of job seekers and circulated them to appropriate businesses, chosen from an employer database.

Advantages and disadvantages of temporary posts

It is clear from statistics already quoted that temporary staff are a significant group in the structure of higher education, acting as a pool of labour from which some members are selected into permanent contracts, while others gain experience and move elsewhere. There are certain advantages for both individual academics and other key players in the growth of temporary contracts in higher education.

- While entry is still highly competitive, the growth in short term posts allows large numbers of postgraduates to test whether an academic career is right for them without undertaking a permanent commitment.
- Academic posts allow staff to remain close to their subject in a way which may not be possible in other occupations, where transferable skills, but not necessarily subject knowledge may be employed.
- Having spent four to seven years in higher education, most contract staff are very comfortable with the university environment and enjoy the life-style and intellectual challenges involved in working in a university community.
- For those who subsequently leave higher education, it generally looks prestigious to have had a university as an employer, although if the period of

employment in higher education has been extensive, doubts may creep in about possible difficulties in making a transition to what some employers consider to be 'the real world'.

- For institutions it is good to have ready availability of well qualified candidates to fill temporary posts. To that extent, the high turn-over rate is not a problem in most disciplines.
- Temporary contracts enable institutions to see the results achieved by staff over the short-term before selecting those who will become the top cadre who secure permanent employment.
- Short term contracts allow institutions to respond quickly if they encounter financial short-falls. Wage bills can be quickly adjusted by simply allowing short-term contracts to expire.
- Funding bodies prefer the focused approach which enables them to track expenditure against the specific projects for which it was allocated.

While there may be more advantages than disadvantages in undertaking a temporary contract in higher education in the early part of a career, difficulties increase for some researchers at a later stage. There are also inefficiencies and uncertainties inherent in this situation for institutions and funding bodies.

- There is ample evidence that many contract research staff do not enjoy parity of employment conditions alongside permanent staff.[12] Through waiver clauses, they may be asked to forego the holiday, sickness benefit and pension entitlements available to permanent staff. At an organisational and social level they are sometimes excluded from staff meetings and departmental strategic planning sessions. These and other differentiations may heighten the sense of being treated as 'second class citizens'.
- Funding constraints and the need to bid competitively in an overcrowded market mean that it can be difficult to make career progress by securing upgrading on the salary scale. Hence the concept which some contract staff have of being 'priced out of the market' because 'I am too expensive'.
- Living with the uncertainty of short term contracts makes it difficult to give a whole-hearted commitment, particularly towards the end of a contract. By that stage there is a very real conflict between the desire to finish the project to a high standard and on time and the self preservation instinct to spend time seeking the next job.
- The combination of insecure and generally fairly low income is not appealing to banks, building societies and other potential lenders. It can therefore be difficult for contract staff to secure mortgages or arrange credit. If a partner is also a contract researcher, a student or not in employment, the situation is compounded.
- Although it is perfectly normal to proceed through an academic career via a large number of short contracts, this can produce a CV which gives an impression of instability, particularly if it is punctuated by periods of

unemployment while waiting for a contract to come through. This pattern may not be understood by other employers if a contract researcher or tempo-rary lecturer tries to switch to a career outside academia.

- The level of commitment exhibited by contract staff in these circumstances is normally amazingly high, but there is always a concern for academic departments that necessity will oblige temporary staff to devote time to job-seeking as a contract nears its end. The worst possible scenario is to be left with a project which is a couple of months short of completion, at which point it becomes difficult to recruit within such a tight timescale an appro-priate person who is capable of seeing the project through to the end, only for that person to be dismissed when the funding runs out.

- For personnel officers the constant turnover of staff on short term contracts is both time-consuming and costly. An institution with a large research base may issue as many as 3,000 contracts per year to temporary academic staff, some of whom may be on monthly renewable contracts. When labour costs are added to running costs for such an exercise, it is not the most efficient way of running an institution, but personnel officers are locked into this method because of the way in which funding comes in from external sources.

- The highly-focused approach dictated by tight funding and short timescales does not always produce the best research. Promising avenues at a tangent to the main research topic may not be explored, thus resulting in the loss of potentially signif-icant discoveries or outcomes. Safe routes to end products rather than more imaginative ones with an element of risk attached will generally be preferred, but these are not always those which lead to the greatest expansion of knowledge.

For the individual it is a matter of personal decision as to whether the advan-tages out-weigh the disadvantages. The exercises in part II of the book are designed to help in that decision-making process.

Part I has set the scene for the remainder of the book. It has explained the nature and causes of changes in the staffing structure of universities. It has also shown that several interested parties have a strong motivation to take steps to address the career development needs of contract research staff, with potential long term benefits for other groups of academic and professional staff within higher education. To this extent, the unified UK higher education system gives greater cause for hope of a co-ordinated approach to the optimum deployment of academic researchers than is the case in a similar situation in the USA, where there is no central impetus towards addressing the issue of a surplus of academic researchers because there is no single higher education system in operation because of the diversity of funding arrangements.

Finally, however, whatever support and facilities are provided, each person is ultimately responsible for his or her own career development. Part II of this book is therefore designed to help readers to work through various stages of a structured approach to career planning, beginning with self-assessment and ending with a polished interview performance when applying for an academic or an alternative job.

Part II

Focus on yourself

Chapter 2

Developing your career plan

You are reading this book in the light of the very competitive labour market in higher education and you may be debating whether you have the desire or ability to stay on track towards an academic career. This may be because you recognise how few academic jobs exist in your field and how intensely keen the competition is for such vacancies. Perhaps you have already had some temporary contracts in lecturing, researching or tutoring, but hesitate to take further short-term posts because of practical concerns such as low income and the problems associated with obtaining a mortgage. Alternatively, you may have decided there are aspects of academic life which do not fully engage your talents and interests. You may wish to transfer some of your academic skills to another setting to develop your career in a different context.

The purpose of this book is not to persuade you to pursue a career in any particular field but to enable you to see that you have a variety of options for your future career. The exercises are designed to help you to weigh up the pros and cons of these options and to reach a balanced decision on the route you want to take now. If after making the assessment you decide the academic route is the most suitable option for you, the book will have served its purpose. Equally, if you decide to move out of academic life, your decision to do so will be based on sound reasons and you will know why you have made this choice and why it is the best one for you at this time.

Steps in planning your career

What you are doing now – the reassessment of your career options and taking these forward into the job hunt – is a series of activities you will probably repeat several times in your working life. The model below (Figure 2.1), first detailed by A. G. Watts, describes what you need to do to achieve a result appropriate for the next phase of your career.[1]

In Part II of this book we shall explore self awareness and opportunity awareness in some detail and move on to the decision making process. The skills required for effective 'transition' – that is, securing a job offer through appropriate contact with employers – will be examined in Part IV.

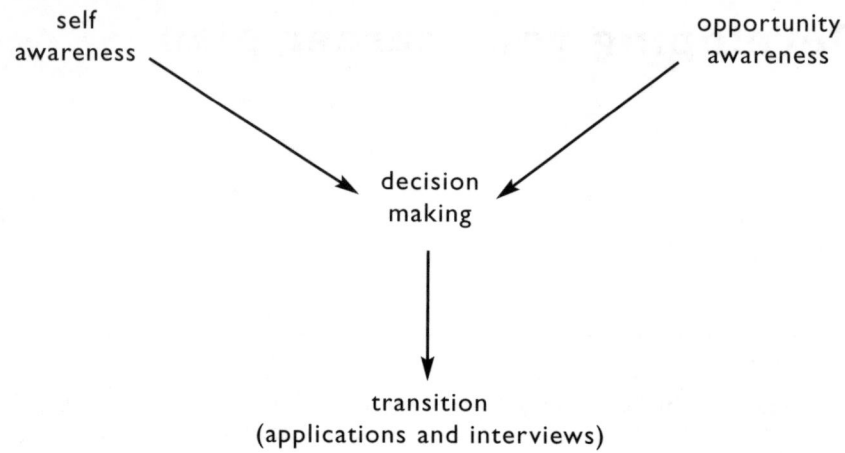

Figure 2.1 Career choice process

Unless you are particularly fortunate, you will probably need to work through this model several times before you are successful in your job hunt. For example, no matter how thorough you are in your investigations, it may not be until you have an employer interview that you understand fully the nature of that job in that particular organisation.

Examples

George had decided to move out of his contract research job in biology and to move into industry by developing his strong computer programming skills. On attending a pre-interview visit to a company, he realised the job would involve him in dealing with clients on a face to face basis. He had to return to the self-assessment stage to look for evidence to help him decide if he would like to do this and would be able to do it well, before he took his application further.

Morven had applied for jobs in personnel and training as she had particularly enjoyed mentoring Ph.D. students. After being rejected for a training post, she asked for feedback from the employer. She was told she had appeared to be more interested in the needs of the individual than the needs of the organisation and that while there is always a balance between the two in personnel management, the needs of the organisation must come first. This encouraged Morven to reassess her knowledge of this type of work and to consider teaching in schools as an option.

So each of the steps in the model informs and affects the other steps. Changing your career is not in reality a straight forward linear development. It could be described as a network of trains shunting back and forward, each move affecting all the other trains, but the total movement is forward.

Understanding the career choice process

Career choice is clearly a very personal process, depending on all the influences on your life so far, and it can be approached in the same logical manner that you would apply to your academic research. Theorists have long analysed the process of choice to identify the factors which influence career paths. All theories recognise that the blend of factors, how they interrelate and how they influence decision making, is unique for each individual. These factors come not only from our individual make up and past experiences, but also from outside influences, including our personal circumstances, the changing nature of the job market and the economic climate.

The factors which will determine career options are simplified in the following diagram (Figure 2.2).

Influences on your potential

Internal factors

These are the factors over which you have most control. There are many ways to organise the description of these, but for the purposes of this book we can group them as:

- your interests – what you enjoy doing
- your skills – what you do well
- your values – what gives meaning to your work
- your temperament – including how you relate to others, your emotional world, and your style of thinking.

Taken on their own, these factors can describe an 'ideal' job and workplace for

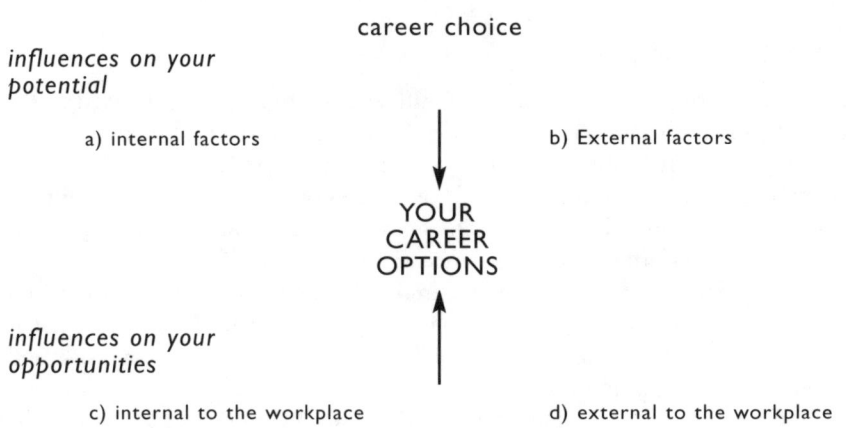

Figure 2.2 Factors influencing career options

you, a kind of black and white picture which is quickly coloured by factors personal to you.

External factors

Other factors affecting your potential involve your needs from work in terms of your personal circumstances. These can include your financial circumstances (e.g. your need to pay a mortgage) but also limitations (or opportunities!) imposed by the expectations others might have of you (e.g. to 'use' your subject) and the personal responsibilities you may have (e.g. geographical location in relation to children's schooling).

Influences on your opportunities

These factors are related to the world outside your sphere of influence and generally you will have less control over how they affect your career options. (Of course, if you decide to move into politics or government administration, you may be in a position to influence these factors in the long term!).

Internal to the workplace

These factors include the skills required for particular jobs in particular organisations, the qualifications and experiences expected and the training opportunities available. In the process of career choice, these influences will bring our coloured two-dimensional picture into relief. As well as influencing career choice, these factors can determine the steps and pace you need to take to move into your chosen option. For example, if you have a skills gap you may need to seek training or experience to fill that gap.

External to the workplace

These include the direct and indirect influences which governments have – nationally and internationally – in determining the nature of job opportunities. For example, the insecurity of the position of contract researchers in this country may be viewed as the indirect result of policies of successive governments in the funding of research. Economic factors have a strong bearing on major trends in employment and influence the balance of types of work likely to be available. Wider sociological factors may imply certain pressures on you to conform in a particular way; for example you must have a 'graduate' career (however that is defined). New technologies are constantly producing new types of work and reducing opportunities in other fields.

All of the factors in the diagram will have some effect on your career choice. It is a simple model of what is in reality a very complex process. Career choice in today's world can never be seen as a simple matching process, matching your personal factors with those which the employer is seeking. There will never be a perfect fit. Your task in the chapters which follow is to identify those factors which are significant for you, to weigh them in the balance and to find the 'best' fit at present. The factors do not sit independently of each other, but interlink, creating cause and effect, and are frequently changing.

As you explore the exercises in the following chapter try to bear in mind the following broad principles which apply to the process of career choice at this time.

- Most of us could do a wide range of jobs well, and gain satisfaction from doing them. You are not, therefore, seeking the single 'right' job for you; the ideal exists in only the very rarest of cases. Your task is to identify that broad range of jobs in the market place which reasonably fits your criteria.
- The combination of factors which affect your choices now is unique to this time in your life. It follows that any choice made now may need to be reviewed at some later stage in your working life. In other words, the business of career planning is a process in which you will need to keep involved as you gain new skills, have new life experiences, and as your circumstances change. In addition to these personal developments, the forces in the market place are likely to continue to change according to world economic and political movements and the advent of new technologies.
- It is unreasonable to expect any job to fulfil all your needs; there will always be some element of compromise. You may need to explore other ways of satisfying some aspects of yourself, through voluntary work or outside interests, for example.
- You are the expert on what you want and what you have to offer. The best person to gather and analyse the information which will influence your decisions is yourself.
- Job titles can be meaningless (e.g. 'administrative officer'). Many jobs which are advertised will never be found in a careers directory, and many jobs are never advertised. If you develop a clear template of what is important for you, you will be in a position to measure the suitability of the jobs you are exploring.
- You will often hear of someone who makes a really exciting career move and puts it down to luck, luck at being in the right place at the right time, or in having the right contacts in the field. Try to adopt the principle that 'luck is no more than preparation meeting opportunity'. You should take responsibility for preparing the circumstances which will create your own luck.

Your options

Before looking in detail at self assessment, let us explore the broad options open to you and begin to measure their suitability. There are three ways forward:

- linear progression – continuing in the research field of your subject

- developing a thread of existing expertise, such as computing skills or interviewing skills
- taking a new direction.

Figures 2.3, 2.4 and 2.5 outline some of the possibilities. Add any others which come to mind. Circle those which seem possible routes for you at this time, bearing in mind what we have just outlined about the process.

The exercises you will complete in the next chapters may help you to understand why these seem possibilities at this time, helping to confirm or change your preferences.

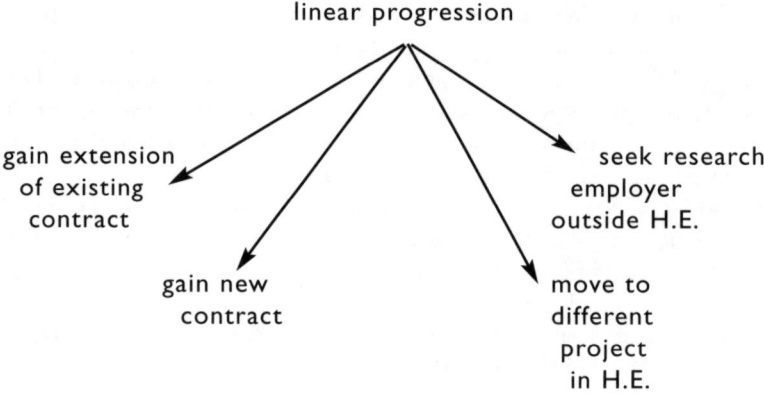

Figure 2.3 Moving forward: linear progression

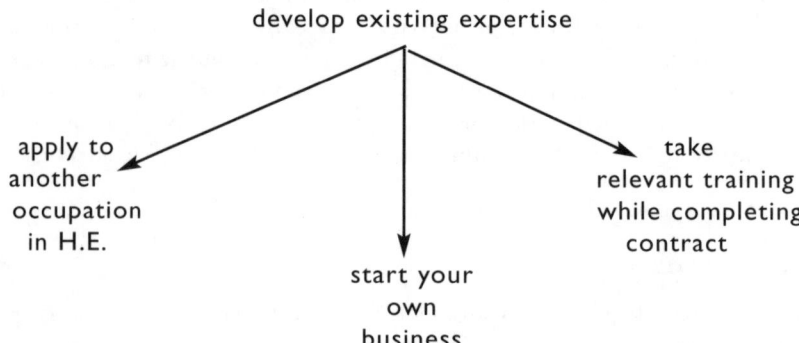

Figure 2.4 Moving forward: developing existing expertise

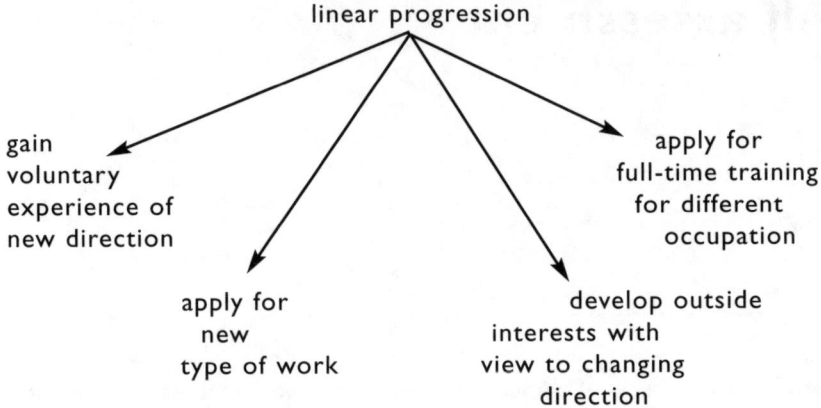

Figure 2.5 Moving forward: new direction

Chapter 3

Self assessment

Central to the process of choice is the collection and analysis of information about each of the sets of factors as they relate to you. As the options you choose must be 'user friendly' in providing some sort of job satisfaction, it seems logical to start with the internal personal factors and complete a self assessment of these. For these factors you are the expert, you know yourself better than anyone else. Sometimes, however, our self-knowledge and perception are clouded, (e.g. by the stress of having to make a decision, or a difficult experience at work, or lack of relevant experiences), so it can be useful to discuss your assessments with someone who knows you well. Any light thrown on how others see you will provide more depth to the picture you build up of yourself. The exercises in this chapter are designed to help you build up this picture. They are tools which will help you to embark on your thinking about the issues which are important to you.

Note Sometimes, faced with a blank questionnaire it is difficult to start. Remember you are not making firm commitments as yet; use a pencil so you can make changes at a later stage.

Tapping your self knowledge

As we have seen in chapter 2, the personal factors involved in career choice can be described as your skills, interests, values, and temperament as well as the external factors involving your personal circumstances.

The factors are all interlinked and the total picture is dependent on all of them.

The relationship of personal factors in career choice is complex and unique for each of us at any stage in our lives. The simple jigsaw attempts to clarify how this operates.

- For each of us the shape of the picture is different; for example, none of us would see our own factors fitting into a neat square box! There will always be ragged unfinished edges which change over time.
- The way the pieces fit together is unique and may change over time.

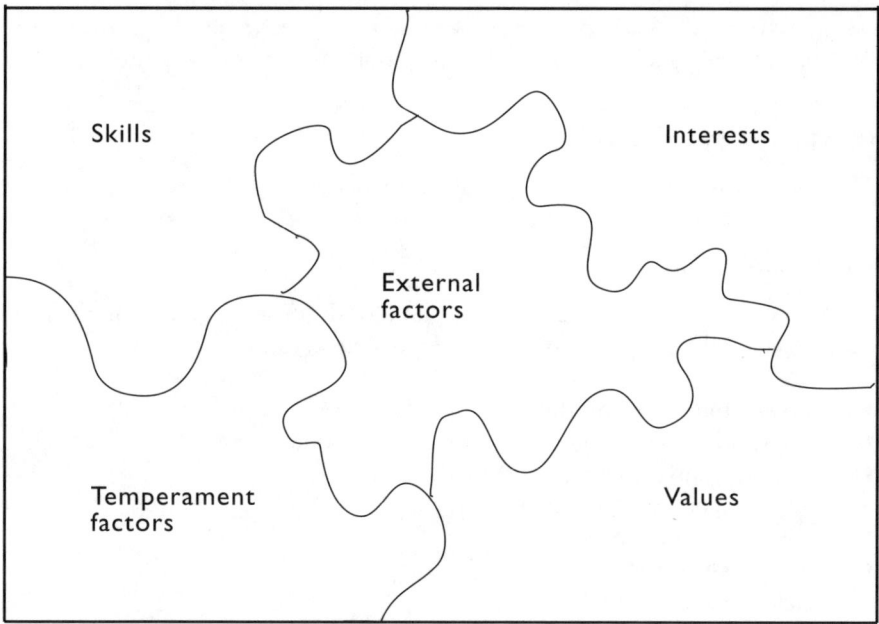

Figure 3.1 Personal factors in career choice

- The relative importance of each group of factors is unique and may also change over time.
- To gain a complete picture all the factors must be considered, but as with any jigsaw, it really does not matter in which order the pieces are put together.

We shall explore each of these groups of factors separately and then consider how they fit together for you as an individual.

Skills

What do we mean by 'skills' or 'abilities' or 'capabilities'? These are all expressions which are used to describe this group of factors. A great deal has been written in recent years about skills by academics, employers and careers advisers, but it can appear that they all have rather different, unexpressed, definitions of what is meant by the term 'skill.' For our purposes we define it as that which demonstrates what an individual can do and the level at which it can be performed. Such skills can be learnt (driving a car, for example) or be derived from natural aptitude, such as manual dexterity. The highest level of skill is likely to be achieved where a natural aptitude has been developed through learning, for example, written communication. Skills can be specific to a particular context, or be transferable to other contexts. Too often we fail to recognise the transferability of our skills. A particular scientific technique may have limited application, while working co-operatively with others to develop the same technique can show well developed team working skills which can be transferred to other contexts.

Identifying your skills

The first step is to identify current and past experiences.

Work related skills

Focus on your work experience over the past month (or similar period in the past which has involved typical tasks). During that time, have you:

- worked alone or with others?
- conducted research on primary or secondary sources?
- analysed statistical data?
- written reports or a section of your thesis?
- attended a conference?
- debated issues with colleagues?
- taught undergraduates?
- set up a computer model or a database?
- persuaded someone to provide access to facilities or sources of information?
- re-negotiated a deadline?
- encountered problems and tried to resolve them?
- suffered set backs and had to be resilient?
- interviewed subjects?

There will be many other activities you can identify. This will help you to recognise the complexity of your current work, in a degree of detail which may not be immediately evident to non-academic employers. Another way to do this is to consider a project you have completed. What activities did this involve? Write down as much detail as you can.

Exercise

Now make a list of your activities in the left hand column of Exercise 3.1 and in the right hand column extrapolate the skills you display in tackling each activity. Spend some time doing this. You want to be as detailed as possible.

Which of all these work related skills are very specific to your current job and are unlikely to be transferable to another context? Consider this carefully. You may wish to discuss it with someone who knows you well. It is important to list these skills in detail, they are a strong part of your marketing strategy for a further academic post or similar occupation. This is what will make you stand out in front of other candidates for such posts. We will look again at the more transferable skills in a later exercise.

Exercise 3.1 Example

Activity	Skills
Debating with colleagues	Analyses of complex issues, listening skills, persuasive skills, communication skills

Exercise 3.1 Work related skills

Activity	Skills

Other skills

Now consider your experiences more widely, in your life outside work and further back in time. Can you identify evidence of other skills which you have developed? These may be in need of formal development or revived from a dormant state, such as writing for a student newspaper (Exercise 3.2).

You now have a list of all your transferable and specific skills. Whatever options you choose, this is a starting point to provide evidence of your skill profile to future employers. The next step is to define the level of skills you have achieved for each of these. This can be difficult where you are asked to measure yourself against something which has not been formally tested. The

Exercise 3.2 Example

Activity	Skills
Student newspaper editor	• Writing for a specific audience • Leadership skills • Meeting deadlines

Exercise 3.2 Skills developed outside of work

Activity	Skills

one measure you have is a comparison with your peers. For example, you can ask yourself the questions, 'If I compare my presentation skills (or any other you choose) with those of others I have observed making similar presentations, how well do I perform and can I think of examples to demonstrate this?'

Transferable skills can be described in many ways. Here we define some of the broad categories which reflect the kind of skills employers look for.

*   Verbal communication includes communicating with others on a one to one basis (telephone and face to face) in small groups, large groups.
*   Written communication involves writing to suit different media, including lecture notes, reports, articles, theses.
*   Interpersonal skills include a range of skills involving persuading, influencing, leading, teaching, interviewing others.

- Numeracy skills. These are not mathematical skills but involve the manipulation of numbers, understanding and interpretation of statistical tables and graphs.
- Information technology. This includes word-processing and e-mail, statistical packages, the Internet, and spreadsheets as well as the sophisticated systems used by many contract researchers.
- Reasoning skills involve analysis, planning, problem solving.

For each of these categories, consider the evidence you have detailed in terms of your work and other activities in relation to your peers. How do you estimate your personal level of skill in each area? If you find this difficult, consult someone who knows you well and is likely to be positive and honest about you.

Verbal communication

Assess your level of skill in the right hand column of Exercise 3.3 using the scale of A to E (see note below exercise).

Exercise 3.3 Verbal communication

Evidence	Level of skills in relation to peers
Be specific in the evidence you provide, e.g. Making presentations (What about? To whom?) Leading tutorials (What about? To whom?) Lecturing (What about? To whom?) Debating (What about? To whom?)	

Note
A = Significantly better than most, B = Better than most, C = About the same as most, D = Poorer than most, E = Significantly poorer than most

Written communication

Assess your level of skill in the right hand column of Exercise 3.4 using the scale of A to E.

Interpersonal skills

Assess your level of skill in the right hand column of Exercise 3.5 using the scale of A to E.

Numeracy

Assess your level of skill in the right hand column of Exercise 3.6 using the scale of A to E.

Information technology

Assess your level of skill in the right hand column of Exercise 3.7 using the scale of A to E.

Reasoning

Assess your level of skill in the right hand column of Exercise 3.8 using the scale of A to E.

Exercise 3.4 Written communication

Evidence	Level of skills in relation to peers
e.g. Making a grant proposal Producing work to deadlines Generating authoritative statements on key issues Writing for different audiences	

Exercise 3.5 Interpersonal skills

Evidence	*Level of skills in relation to peers*

e.g.
Developing a team member
Managing others/motivating others
Delegating
Mentoring
Negotiation/persuasion
Qualitative research
Networking

Exercise 3.6 Numeracy

Evidence	*Level of skills in relation to peers*

e.g.
Planning a budget
Maintaining accounts
Drawing up statistical charts from your
research

Exercise 3.7 Information technology

Evidence	*Level of skills in relation to peers*

e.g.
Preparing spreadsheets for a project
Designing a multimedia presentation
De-bugging a computer program

Exercise 3.8 Reasoning

Evidence	*Level of skills in relation to peers*

e.g.
Planning a project
Solving a problem in your research
Developing a theoretical model based
    on your experience/research

Breaking your skills down in this way will help you produce concrete evidence to employers of your suitability and appropriate levels of skills and experience.

Most jobs require a combination of transferable skills in these categories. The specific combination will vary with each type of work.

Before we leave your skills analysis there are still some questions to answer (Exercise 3.9).

Exercise 3.9 **Preferred skills**

1 You now know where your key skills lie, but which of these would you want to continue with and to be a dominant part of your future jobs? Make some notes.

2 Are there skills you do not want to use in the future, or prefer to have less prominent in your future working life? Make some notes.

3 Are there skills you have not yet developed, but which you would like to be part of your future working life? Make some notes.

Your answers to these questions may provide some clues about whether you wish to continue to work in academic research.

Interests

For the purposes of this book, we define interests as factors which determine what we enjoy in our work, whether it is our main activity or something which we do outside paid employment. Examination of the lists of activities you completed for your skills analysis will help to define your occupational interests.

Look carefully at the activity lists. Which of these do you particularly enjoy doing? Detail them in Exercise 3.10.

Now consider whether there are any common threads to these interests? You may wish to add others to the following categories of interest:

Scientific – physical   Commercial
Scientific – biological   Literary
Artistic   People

Exercise 3.10 Preferred activities

Activities which I enjoy

Exercise 3.11 Preferred interests

Which would you see as your dominant group of interests?

To what extent is it important to you that these interests are satisfied in your work? It is unlikely that any job will fully satisfy your occupational interests. Indeed it could be argued that it is unhealthy to expect a job to do so. When you are fully stretched at work, stress factors can be ameliorated where outside interests provide a release of tensions through a change of focus.
How well are your main interests satisfied in your current work?

Values

For many people, values are the least tangible aspect of self, and therefore the most difficult to define. Very often, those who feel unfulfilled and frustrated by their work are involved in activities and organisations which do not fit with their value system. Values give meaning or worth to our work. Values motivate us and we each operate our own individual value system. These are drawn from our life experiences, the value systems operating in the family, at school, friends and our fields of study and interest.

In terms of career satisfaction, values become more important over time, but the relative importance of particular values can also change over time and is related to changing life circumstances. For example, in the early years after graduation, some people are most strongly motivated by intellectual challenge, or by being involved in something 'worthwhile.' Changing personal circumstances (e.g. family responsibilities or a mortgage), can develop stronger motivators along the lines of financial reward, security or status. It is important to understand there is nothing intrinsically good or bad in any of these value systems; we are all different, all a product of our own life experiences.

As with our occupational interests, it is unlikely that our value systems will be completely satisfied in work and we normally make compromises. Where the nature of the work, the aims of the organisation, or the values of people involved at work are in conflict with our own it is unlikely we will be happy at work. This may in fact be the reason you find yourself reading this book.

So, how can you identify your values? There may be some clues in the lists of skills and interests you completed in the earlier exercises. Even without fully knowing why, you have probably sought work already which meets your values. For example you may have initially taken a job in contract research because of a desire to be with like minded people or a disinclination to work in a commercial field.

Another way to begin to identify your values is to review for yourself the recruitment pages of a number of newspapers. Assume, for the exercise, that you have no constraints, you can work anywhere, you have no financial commitments and you could do whatever appeals to you. Spend time reviewing the advertised vacancies and circle those which, on the face of it, you would really like to do. (It does not matter, for this exercise, if you do not really know what the job advertised involves). Try to find at least a dozen. Once you have your 'fantasy' vacancies, ask yourself for each one, 'What is it about this that really appeals?' Note in Exercise 3.12, the factors that begin to emerge. For example, Penny circled the job 'Director of British Council'. The reasons this appealed to her included: power and influence; using past experience of work overseas; opportunity to make change and a well respected organisation.

When you have done exercise 3.12, check if certain words appear frequently, such as 'status', 'intellectual challenge', 'worthwhile', 'high salary', 'security'. This is a strong message about what is important to you at this time. Try to produce a priority list of your values (Exercise 3.13).

Exercise 3.12 Occupations which appeal

List of jobs/activities	Why this appeals

Exercise 3.13 Values

Key values for me

To what extent are these values satisfied in your current job? (Remember you are measuring this against the ideal, you will almost certainly have to compromise to some extent).

Temperament

Temperament describes the aspects of your personality expressed by the style in which you deal with people or approach tasks. It also influences your feelings and emotions and determines how you react in various situations.

Do Exercise 3.14.

Exercise 3.14 Temperament

Look at the list below and underline any adjectives which seem characteristic of you. Add any others which would describe you.

Adaptable	Adventurous	Assertive	Others
Cautious	Cheerful	Competitive	
Confident	Co-operative	Decisive	
Energetic	Enthusiastic	Imaginative	
Independent	Organised	Persistent	
Reserved	Tactful	Methodical	
Outgoing	Relaxed	Resilient	
Meticulous	Patient	Reliable	
Sensitive	Consistent	Warm	
to others	Objective	Excitable	
Introspective	Changeable	Shy	

It is important to remember that there is nothing intrinsically good or bad about any of the characteristics of temperament on the main list, but they may be more suited to some jobs than to others. For instance, it is appropriate for a sales representative to be competitive but this trait could be misplaced in a social worker. Look also for the hidden strengths behind certain adjectives. For example, someone who is reserved may also be very patient and not liable to upset others by losing their temper. Consider all the plus points in the words you have chosen to describe yourself. It can also be illuminating to understand how others see you, so try to get someone who knows you well to complete the exercise for you.

To what extent are these factors accommodated in your current job?

External factors

Your circumstances

Once again, these are very individual. They depend, for example, on your health, marital status, financial commitments and family responsibilities. They may have a strong link to your value system, for instance, a mortgage and two children might mean you want to seek high security and work based in one place. It is important to acknowledge your own circumstances and assess the influence they might have on your career options. Use Exercise 3.15 to detail these.

The assumption is often made that personal circumstances place limitations on career/job options, but perhaps it is not always so. Try to discuss – with someone who knows you well – just how limiting these factors really are.

To what extent are your circumstances accommodated in your current job?

Exercise 3.15 Personal circumstances

Circumstance	Effect on career options

Summing up

We have now explored your skills, interests, values, temperament and circum-stances. How do these affect your career options? Go back over the exercises and put together a profile of your ideal job using Exercises 3.16 and 3.17.

My ideal job

You should now have a template to use in weighing up broad options, in exploring specific types of work and types of employer. Try not to regard your template as fixed at this point, the more you explore, the clearer this picture will become. Differing circumstances over time will make compromises more or less acceptable.

We will use the factors identified here in generating options in chapter 4 and the decision making process in chapter 6.

Exercise 3.16 Factors in my ideal job

Specific skills

General transferable skills

Interests I would like to be developed

Values I would like to be satisfied

Factors of temperament I should consider

Circumstances which will influence my decision

Exercise 3.17 Review of personal profile

Looking at the picture as a whole, does this fit together? Are there conflicts; for example, do your current skills fit your interests and values?

If there are conflicts, how can you resolve them? For example, by training, voluntary experience and so on?

What are your priorities?

Where would you be prepared to make compromises?

Chapter 4

Generating career ideas

This book is not intended to be a careers encyclopaedia. Such publications exist and you may find them useful in the process of your search. The focus of this chapter is on methods of generating career ideas using your self-assessment in chapter 3. Various methods are described and we conclude with some practical exercises which you can do on your own, or with someone who knows you well, to start the process of generating ideas.

Workbooks

At the simplest level, various workbooks can help you to compare your self-assessment with the profiles of people working in groups of occupations. Most of these are designed for recent graduates, undergraduates or the general population and may not go into sufficient detail for occupations which would interest you, but they could be a useful starting point. Even if suggestions seem unexpected or unlikely, do not necessarily dismiss them out of hand. It could mean that:

- you do not really know what a particular job entails
- you need to review some of your self-assessment.

If you want to try this approach, the following workbooks should be available for reference in most higher education careers services:

Build Your Own Rainbow
What Colour Is Your Parachute?
Managing Your Career
Where Next?

Computer aided career guidance systems (CACGS)

These also operate on a system of matching your characteristics with those which practitioners have indicated are compatible with those of different occupations.

The one most relevant for readers of this book is PROSPECT (HE) as it contains profiles of over 400 occupations, all at graduate level and based on data obtained from practitioners in these fields. It makes a thorough exploration of skills required for various types of the work, entry requirements, training opportunities, competition for entry and sources of information can be accessed for each option. The system is very flexible, and using the self-assessment section can be thought provoking. It is rightly described as a learning system: the user is constantly using the information generated to learn more about themselves and occupations. The outcome of the process for the user is a print-out, showing preferred areas of work and specific occupations which appear to suit their profile.

Access may be restricted because of demand from student users. You should enquire at your university careers service about local arrangements.

Career counselling

At an early stage in your career search you may find it helpful to speak to a careers adviser, who can help you to review your self-assessment objectively and clarify career directions which would be compatible with your skills, interests, values and temperament.

You will gain most from your discussion with a careers adviser if you spend some time before your interview working on the self-assessment exercises in chapter 3.

It is important to understand the nature of the working relationship which you will have with your careers adviser. This is not someone who will persuade or direct you towards certain occupations. The careers adviser's role rather is to facilitate your own thinking and decision making process. In helping you through this process the adviser may:

- listen attentively to what you say and ask you to clarify aspects which are not clear, thus helping you to understand them better yourself
- help you to identify a whole range of inter-connected issues which may be involved in the process of deciding on a career direction
- reflect back to you your own statements, thus bringing out the significance of recurring themes or showing you how your deep seated feelings are mirrored in the vocabulary and the body language which you use
- challenge inconsistencies in your statements, which may force you to review where your real interests and concerns lie
- help you to explore various options and work through the possible advantages and disavantages of taking each route
- ask you to summarise what you have to offer, the nature of your concerns and your attitude towards your various options, thus helping you to formulate conclusions about your thinking on these important issues, which may have been vague up to that point
- act as a sounding board while you commit yourself to take various actions

which will help you to move forward in a carefully determined direction towards your career goal.

All of this is unlikely to happen in a single meeting. For most people the process of moving from self-assessment through exploration of opportunities to decision making and then to self-presentation to employers takes place over a period of time. This may be short or long depending on the amount of time which the individual can commit to the process and the degree of reflection and information gathering required at each stage.

Discussions with an adviser can therefore be interspersed with other activities, such as skills identification exercises, computer aided guidance, reading information booklets, visiting practitioners and reflecting on decision making models. These stages are discussed elsewhere in this book.

If you are a current postgraduate student, you will almost certainly have access to a university careers service and will be able to make an appointment to see a careers adviser, usually someone specialising in giving advice to students in your discipline, but also able to advise on careers suitable for graduates of any discipline.

If you are a recent graduate of a UK university, you should be able to receive some level of help through a reciprocal agreement at most university careers services. Depending on staffing levels, however, this may not always entitle you to a careers interview. Some institutions charge for these services and it is best to ring the careers service in your nearest university to find out about local arrangements.

If you graduated several years ago, not all careers services will be able to offer you an interview because of resource constraints, but it is always worth ringing to enquire about the situation.

Should a careers service be unable to help you, the staff are likely to know of the services locally which offer careers advice on a paid basis. Some of these are operated by local enterprise bodies or similar public sector agencies and these make relatively modest charges for advising adults. Most, however, have a very local emphasis and may have almost no experience of working with clients at post-doctoral level.

The other alternative is private careers counsellors; details can be found in *Yellow Pages*, but be sure to ask about charges before making an appointment as some can be expensive. Sometimes these counsellors are associated with recruitment and placement agencies. It is illegal for recruitment agencies to charge job seekers and their income is derived from payments by employers. In beginning the process of matching you with suitable employers, recruitment consultants may help you to clarify where you are most likely to be successful, but they are not careers advisers and you should not expect them to take you through a career decision making process.

Working out some initial ideas

Workbooks, computers and careers advisers simply facilitate your own thinking on careers; eventually you will decide what route you will follow. At first your thinking on the matter may be quite limited, but as you explore more widely and find out about more career options, you will become more adept at weighing up the possibilities in relation to your own criteria on what you are seeking.

It is never too soon to begin the process of broadening your thinking and the next exercise will help you to brainstorm some possible options for career routes.

Example

Martina is a Ph.D. biology student, who has assessed her work-related skills as being strong on investigation and inter-personal relations. Outside of work, she is interested in sport, hill-walking and other outdoor pursuits. Taking her skills and interests as a starting point for thinking about alternative careers, she came up with the following diagram.

Given her interest in outdoor activities and her strength in interpersonal skills, she considered all the options in Figure 4.1 and decided to pursue those occupations which would take her out of the laboratory, but would still value her degree related skills as useful background experience.

Using outdoor pursuits as a key phrase, Martina came up with a different chart, which includes some of the same options listed in Figure 4.1, but added some other possibilities (see Figure 4.2).

Some of the second range of options would take Martina further away from her scientific research background and some would require further training,

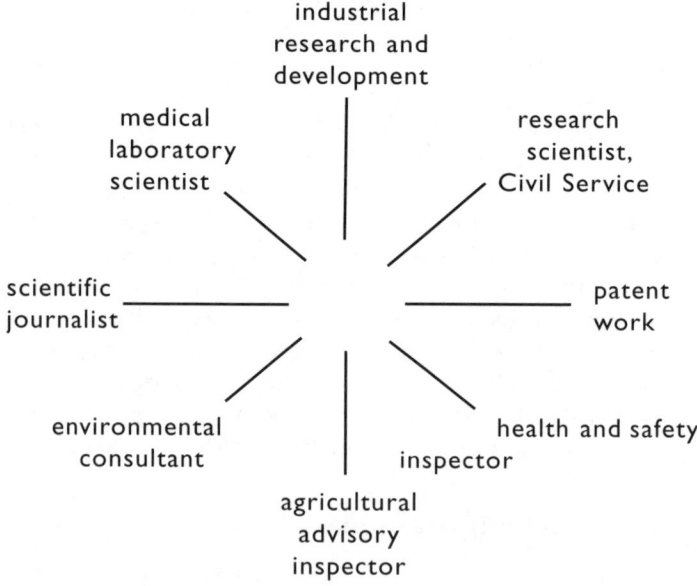

Figure 4.1 Focus on investigative skills

Figure 4.2 Focus on outdoor pursuits

either prior to entry or on the job. These are all considerations which she would have to weigh up before making a decision, but the point is that she could do any of these things if she set her mind to it.

Using this approach, we have drawn up job clusters (Table 4.1) based on some of the key words which contract researchers frequently use in discussions with us. It is not comprehensive, it is meant simply as a prompt for your own thinking when you come to do the exercise yourself.

Exercise

Having seen the outcome of Martina's brainstorming, make your own attempt at Exercises 4.1 and 4.2. You can do this alone, with a partner or in a group.

Use any key words which are significant to you, based on the self-assessment exercise you completed in chapter 3, in the box at the centre of each diagram. We suggest that you may want to use one from your work related skills and one from your wider range of interests, but that is entirely open to you to decide.

Having done these exercises, you may have found several options for which you now wish to obtain further information. Sources of occupational information are suggested in the next chapter.

Alternatively, you may wish to check out your initial brainstorming ideas against other methods of generating career options outlined at the beginning of this chapter. Compare your own thoughts on possible career options with the charts in workbooks and the print-outs from computer guidance systems to see if there are recurring themes. You can also take your diagrams to a

Table 4.1 Job clusters

Problem solving	*Communication*
Management consultancy	Journalism
Civil service administration	Advertising
Marketing	Lobbying organisations
Project management	Publishing
Systems analysis	Public relations
Logistics	Broadcasting
Environmental consultant	Teaching
Systems engineer	Health promotion
	Customer advice for technical products

Analysis	*Debating*
Market research	Sales
Information technology	Marketing
Research and development	Teaching
Accountancy	Community work
Investment analysis	Fund raising
Operational research	Lawyer
Organisation and methods	
Quality control	
Political research	

Exercise 4.1 Work related skills

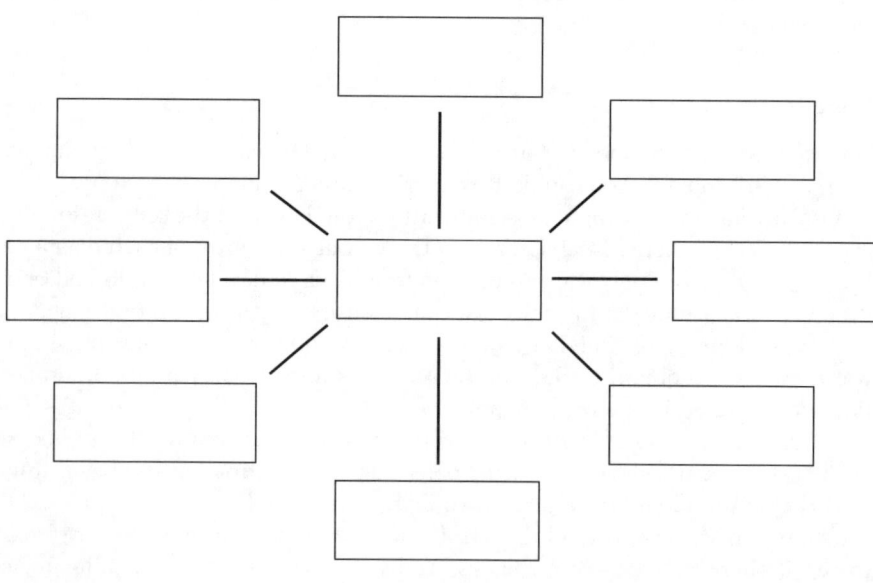

Exercise 4.2 Interests

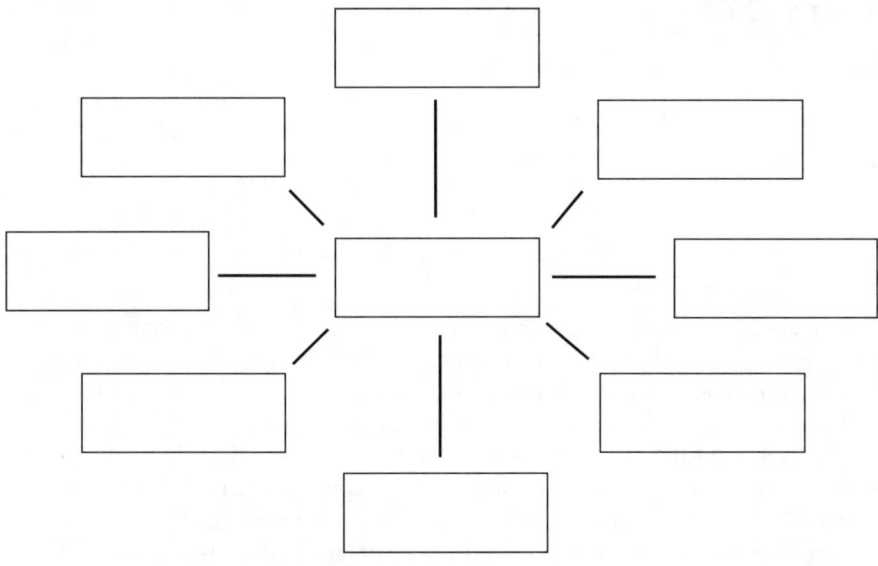

discussion with a careers adviser and examine whether your brainstormed options are compatible with your skills, interests and values and how feasible they might be in terms of any realistic constraints (such as location or re-training costs) and the availability of such employment in the current labour market.

This chapter has demonstrated how lateral thinking around themes which are important to you can produce ideas for career options which you may not have seriously considered, but which are firmly linked to your skills and interests and so are likely to give you job satisfaction. The next chapter explains how you can gather information about various career options before beginning to make decisions on which occupations to pursue.

Chapter 5

Gathering information about careers

Before making a decision on which career to pursue, you need to have sufficient information to weigh up the advantages and disadvantages of a specific occupation for you. There is a wealth of sources of occupational information which can tell you about a whole range of aspects of particular careers.

Before consulting any of these sources, be clear what it is that you wish to know about occupations in order to be able to compare them with one another and with the criteria which you have identified in previous chapters as being important for your circumstances and job satisfaction. This is a matter of individual choice. For instance, for one job seeker the likely pattern of working hours in an occupation may be of considerable importance whereas for another person in different circumstances this factor may be completely insignificant.

Exercise

In Exercise 5.1 draw up your own checklist of points which you wish to clarify about the occupations which you intend to investigate. This may include some of the following items.

- What is the day to day content of the occupation?
- How varied is the content in a typical day, in a month, from year to year?
- What proportion of the time is spent, for example, in contact with other people, on your own, in meeting, etc?
- Of what nature is the contact with people, for example advising, directing, negotiating, instructing?
- What skills are required for this occupation, for example data analysis, numeracy, teamwork, communication skills?
- What temperament is required for this occupation, for example even-tempered, extrovert, willingness to take risks?
- What degree of mobility does the work require, for example a one off re-location, occasional business trips, constant travelling?
- What working hours and conditions are likely to be involved, and what impact is that likely to have on your social and family life?

- What are the pre-entry requirements, and how flexible are these?
- Is there provision for in-service professional development?
- Are there constraints for people with physical or sensory disabilities?
- Are there issues about upper or lower age limits?
- What is the salary, on entry and after five years?
- What are promotion prospects likely to be?

In Exercise 5.1, select from this list the factors which you wish to check and add any others which are significant to you.

Once you have a list drawn up, you can turn your attention to the following sources of information.

Exercise 5.1 Significant factors in an occupation

Occupation	Information required
e.g. Journalism	Is a postgraduate course necessary, or is direct entry possible? What are initial starting salaries and future prospects?

Sources of information

Higher education careers services

The most obvious source of information is higher education careers services. If you are a current student, you will have access to the careers information room in your university careers service. The same is likely to be true if you are a recent graduate. If you no longer live close to the university from which you graduated, you will find that your closest university probably has a reciprocal arrangement with your own university to let recent graduates use their information room. There may occasionally be a small charge for the use of this facility.

If you graduated some time ago, the situation is less clear-cut. Contact your nearest university careers service to find out about your eligibility and directions to other sources of careers information if they are unable to assist you due to resource constraints.

The holdings of information rooms vary depending on the resources available to each careers service. Some are very elaborate, with various on-line computer systems, while others are more basic. Many careers services have World Wide Web pages outlining their facilities and providing a certain level of information. You can expect to find at least some of the following resources in most careers services.

Labour market information

Most higher education careers services hold valuable information on the labour market. This can help you to decide whether a move in a particular direction would be viable.

One of the most useful overviews of the labour market is *Graduate Market Trends*, published by the Higher Education Careers Services Unit (CSU). This quarterly publication gives succinct summaries of various regular and ad-hoc economic surveys. It also interprets CSU's own statistics on graduate vacancies by type of work, type of occupation, degree discipline sought, location and salaries. While based chiefly on vacancies for first time graduate job seekers, these statistics give a good impression of the relative buoyancy of various sectors of the graduate labour market which can be used as a guide by those seeking entry at a more senior level.

Occupational information profiles and booklets

These are produced by the Association of Graduate Careers Advisory Services (AGCAS) on a wide range of occupations entered by graduates. These booklets are researched and written by professional careers advisers, based on national graduate destination statistics, interviews with current practitioners and information supplied by professional bodies and employers. They contain descriptions of occupations, details of qualities and qualifications required for entry, suggestions on routes into each field, training and career prospects and they include bibliographies and contact addresses for further information. Occupational profiles are briefer documents with key information on some of the same issues.

These booklets are available for loan or reference in all university careers services. They may also be purchased from the Higher Education Careers Services Unit (CSU), Prospects House, Booth St. East, Manchester, M13 9EP.

Occupational folders

In addition to information booklets most higher education careers services have reference folders on occupations in which they have built up further information to supplement the booklets. This may include comparative surveys of courses offering professional training, literature from professional bodies, relevant articles and sometimes personal accounts from alumni who have entered particular occupations. These folders point readers to sources of further information if they want to pursue a subject in greater depth.

Computer aided guidance systems

Some of the more advanced computer aided guidance systems (such as PROSPECT HE) not only generate suggestions for suitable occupations, but also contain profiles of them. These give basic details on entry requirements (in terms of qualifications, experience and age limits), the level of competition for entry, salary ranges, sources of vacancies and contacts for further information.

Employers' literature

Although primarily intended to attract you to apply to a particular organisation, employers' literature can also be helpful at an earlier stage in your career search, when you are trying to find out the 'flavour' of an occupation. Many employers' brochures contain descriptions of particular occupations and personal profiles of graduates doing such work. For instance, you could dip into the brochures of a few employers in a particular sector to find out more about investment banking, management consultancy or logistics.

Many employers, especially those in the technology sector, have extensive Web sites which give information not only on recruitment, but on products and services and on the organisation's performance. This can be a useful source of background information.

Other reference materials

Depending on the extent of their resources, careers services may also have a collection of reference books, CD-ROMs and videos on certain occupations. Seek the advice of the careers information manager to make best use of the available stock. The information manager may also be able to refer you to appropriate sources beyond the career service.

Other careers services

Outside the universities there is a network of local careers companies throughout the UK. Some may offer a complete range of services entirely free of charge, while others give some free services plus others with a charge. Nearly all give free access to basic careers information and usually a brief introductory interview is also free.

Unlike higher education careers services, careers companies have to carry information on a much wider range of occupations suitable for people with few or no qualifications right up to those with degrees. They are less likely to carry in-depth information on the whole range of careers for very highly qualified graduates, but their materials may be a useful starting place if you cannot access a university careers service.

Another source is private careers counsellors, listed in *Yellow Pages*. Most of these operate on the basis of individual consultations rather than providing an information centre on open access. Charges are variable, may be on a sliding scale, and should be checked before arranging a consultation.

Libraries

It is possible to obtain a limited range of careers information from most public libraries. If you use this source of information, be very careful to check the dates of publications. Careers information tends to have a short shelf life. Higher education careers services tend not to keep publications which are more than three years old, or much less in the case of information booklets and employers' literature. The same policy may not apply in public libraries where only a limited portion of the budget is devoted to updating careers materials.

City public libraries tend to have a good stock of the types of directories mentioned in the sources of further information listed at the end of this book. If, however, you have access only to a smaller public library, you should be able to request any of the recommended directories through inter-library loan for a small charge.

Professional bodies

Many professional bodies employ education, information or careers officers to produce literature and maintain Web sites on entry to their profession and subsequent career prospects. Their remit may also include answering individual enquiries from prospective entrants to the profession.

Not every occupation has a professional body of this kind, but it is worth checking to see if the field which you plan to enter is affiliated to such an organisation. A good source of information on professional bodies is a directory entitled *British Qualifications*. (See sources of further information.)

Networking

The best source of information on what it is like to work in a particular occupation is practitioners themselves. Ultimately, all other sources of information are based on this resource. Information booklets and computer aided guidance systems are derived from careers advisers' interviews with practitioners. After using booklets and computers as a route into thinking about an occupation, you may want to gain a first hand impression by contacting practitioners for further background information.

If you do this, it is ideal to speak to more than one person to avoid obtaining a biased viewpoint. First hand information is excellent, but you have to be aware that you may be speaking to either an evangelist who can see nothing wrong in the job, or a disgruntled practitioner whose lack of progress may not be typical of the profession. There is therefore an advantage in using the 'neutral' information gathered by careers advisers as well as the 'first person experience' of practitioners.

You may have an initial hesitancy about approaching practitioners for information and advice on their profession, but very rarely does anyone object to giving a little time to speak with a seriously interested potential entrant. After all, the fact that you are interested in their line of work reinforces for practitioners the value of what they are doing.

The following sections will help you to identify who your network contacts might be and what you want to ask them. There are also notes on the etiquette of networking which will help you to overcome any hesitancy you may have about using this technique.

Finding contacts

It may be that you are fortunate enough to know people in the field of work which you propose to enter. This may be the case if you are seeking to move into work closely allied to your area of research. On the other hand, you may not happen to have a facilities manager or an investment analyst in your circle of acquaintances. What can you do then to find appropriate contacts?

When you do not have a direct contact, you may need to explore via other people the routes to finding a practitioner in the field which interests you. There are many starting points for such a quest. Examples are given in Figure 5.1.

The possibilities are virtually endless. Here is a list of some of the more obvious starting points:

People in your department	Professional bodies
Relatives	People whom you meet at conferences
Friends	Personnel officers
Former colleagues	Suppliers
Former employers	Librarians
Alumni	Careers advisers

In Exercise 5.2 write down the names of individuals whom you could contact in

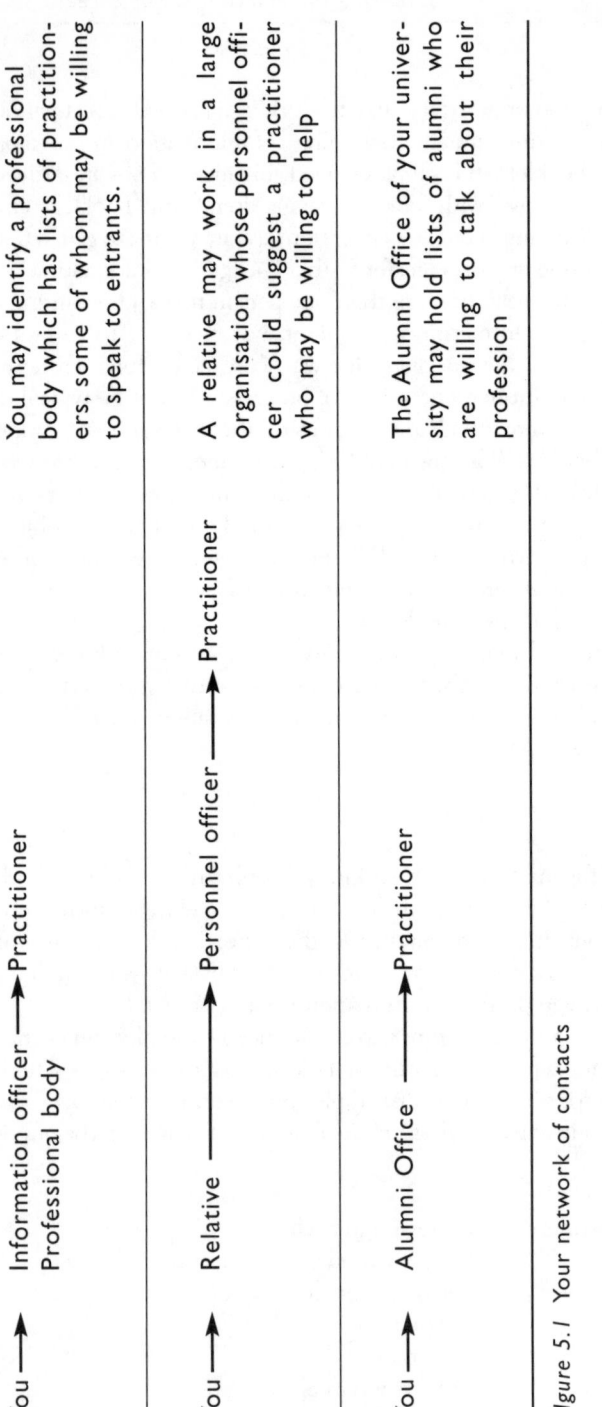

You ⟶ Information officer ⟶ Practitioner
Professional body

You may identify a professional body which has lists of practitioners, some of whom may be willing to speak to entrants.

You ⟶ Relative ⟶ Personnel officer ⟶ Practitioner

A relative may work in a large organisation whose personnel officer could suggest a practitioner who may be willing to help

You ⟶ Alumni Office ⟶ Practitioner

The Alumni Office of your university may hold lists of alumni who are willing to talk about their profession

Figure 5.1 Your network of contacts

order to find more information or further contacts for the occupation which you are trying to explore.

Deciding what to ask

It is frustrating for a busy person to have set time aside to talk to a supposedly eager questioner only to find that the visitor seems very vague about what they want to know. If you have secured time with a practitioner, the least you can do is to be well organised with sensible questions. Review the list of questions which you drew up earlier in this chapter and, in Exercise 5.3, add any others which you might wish to ask someone in the occupation which interests you.

Exercise 5.2 Building your network

Occupation:		
Contact	*Address*	*Tel. no.*

Exercise 5.3 Questions for your contacts

Key questions

Ways of viewing the job at first hand

Contact with a practitioner can take many forms. You will obviously have to be guided by what is convenient for the person who is giving up time to speak to you. Nonetheless, it is useful for you to know about some of the methods of finding out about occupations at first hand which other people have found useful.

One to one conversation

This is the most likely form of contact with a practitioner. If the person meeting you has a very hectic schedule at work and is constantly interrupted, it may be impossible to meet you during working hours. If that is the case, you may feel it is appropriate to offer to take your contact for a coffee or a meal after work. The information gained in this way will be valuable and possibly your contact may be more relaxed and able to spend more time with you.

On the other hand, meeting a practitioner away from the work place means that you do not gain a sense of what the work environment is like. Are the surroundings plush or spartan? Is the atmosphere charged with a bustling sense of activity, or is the pace slow and serene? What kind of office or work space does your practitioner have? What impression do you have of relations between work colleagues? So much information can be gleaned from your impressions of all these surrounding factors that it is better, if possible, to meet your contact at work in order to expand your understanding of what such a job is likely to entail.

Work shadowing

If there are no security issues and if your practitioner has no objections, it may be possible to arrange a brief work shadowing placement. This would enable you to go along with a practitioner as he or she goes about a typical day or week, observing what it is like to work in that occupation and organisation. Not all jobs are suited to this approach and so be guided by your contact in the profession. For instance, if a job entails long spells of writing reports or computer programming, there is not much to be observed over long periods of time. On the other hand, if an occupation involves a wide variety of activities in the course of a day, it is easier to understand the mental agility and stamina required for the job if you have experienced a day in it.

If you have an opportunity to work-shadow, try to identify in advance what you want to find out from your observations and record your findings to help you in your decision making process. As you cannot interrupt your practitioner in full flight during the working day, clarify in advance when would be a suitable time (e.g. over lunch or at the end of the day) for you to ask the questions which will no doubt spring to mind as a result of your observations.

Other 'on the job' experiences

For a better understanding of some jobs, practitioners may be able to point you to activities which are open to the public. For instance, if you are interested in industrial relations, as a member of the public you can sit in on an industrial tribunal hearing. Likewise, there may be public meetings on environmental issues. Your contact may also be able to arrange for you to attend a shareholders' meeting to gain a broad overview of a company's progress.

Such opportunities do not arise in every type of work, but it is certainly worth asking your contacts if there are any activities of this kind which would extend your knowledge of the issues in the profession which you are exploring.

The etiquette of networking

The etiquette of networking follows the simple rules of common courtesy, but in case of doubt, it may be helpful to set out a few guidelines.

Do:

- refer to any intermediary contact who has put you in touch with the practitioner
- set out clearly what you hope to gain from the interview
- indicate realistically how much time you are asking for (half an hour may be reasonable for an initial interview)
- fit in with a time and meeting place to suit the practitioner
- be punctual for the meeting
- phone in advance and explain the reason for any unavoidable delay or cancellation
- come to the interview armed with intelligent questions
- remember to write and thank the practitioner for spending time with you.

Do not:

- be unrealistic about how much time a busy practitioner can spend with you
- keep cancelling and re-arranging appointments
- stray greatly over the time which you requested, unless the practitioner volunteers to do so
- be unrealistic about the range of information which a single practitioner can give you (e.g. on up to date entry requirements)
- ask questions of an intrusive nature
- wear out your welcome by acting like an inquisitor!

The sample letter of introduction (Figure 5.2) indicates how you might approach a potential contact.

Organising information

Gathering information is an essential part of the exploration phase of the career choice process, but if it all sits in a dusty pile on your coffee table, not much will have been achieved. Once your career decision is made, you will have occasion to access careers information again and again while you are in the process of writing applications and preparing for interviews. Information retrieval is therefore just as important as information gathering.

It is a good idea at the outset to begin a careers file or folder, divided into sections for the various occupations which you are investigating. Typical contents of each section may include:

- a print-out on an occupation from PROSPECTS (HE)
- an AGCAS information booklet on an occupation
- a professional body's careers literature
- relevant press cuttings on topics of current interest in a profession
- notes made after an interview with a practitioner
- details of appropriate training courses

42, Chistlebury Avenue
Chesterly
Chiltonshire, CH12 9BT

Mr David Martin
Investments Department
Shield Insurance plc
Westerton
Avonshire, WE14 7XZ   21st December, 1999

Dear Mr Martin,

I write as a result of a conversation with your colleague, Ms Sandra Brown, who was a guest speaker at a conference at the University of Chesterbury, where I am currently a research assistant in the Developing Economies Unit. She kindly gave me your name as a contact for information on careers in investment analysis. I believe that in the interval she may have mentioned my intention to write to you for advice.

When my contract comes to an end next August, I propose to change my career direction and in recent months I have been investigating occupations which would use the research skills which I have developed in my higher degree studies and current post. A further essential requirement is finding an occupation which will provide intellectual stimulus and an opportunity to keep up to date with current affairs. Investment analysis appears to match my criteria and I am now eager to find out more about this type of work from a practitioner. In particular I should like to know more about the nature of the work in a typical week or month and the current prospects of entry to this field.

If you could spare half an hour at a time and place convenient to you, I shall be grateful for any information which you can give me on investment analysis and the likelihood of someone with my background being able to enter this occupation. A copy of my CV is enclosed to give you information on my career to date.

When you have had an opportunity to read this letter and enclosure, I shall call you to see if it would be convenient for us to meet at some point in the next few weeks. With thanks for considering this request.

Yours sincerely,

(Miss) Miranda Cassells

Figure 5.2 Sample letter of introduction

- typical vacancy adverts for this career area
- your summary notes on qualities, skills, qualifications and experience required.

As you become clearer about your ranking of preferred occupations, you may decide not to pursue some occupations which you initially considered. In order to keep control over the volume of information, you may then decide to remove certain sections from your master file and either keep them in a separate file if it is possible that you may reconsider them later, or discard them if you are convinced that they are not suitable or feasible for you.

Keeping such a file is useful for another reason. For most people the process of career choice and finding employment is a fairly lengthy one and it is easy to become down-hearted because change and success do not come overnight. Your well-organised file can serve as a tangible reminder that you are making progress and coming closer every day to making a successful transition into the next phase of your career.

Chapter 6

Decision making

At some point information gathering must cease and decisions have to be made. It is good to have more than one option, but pursuing too many can become unmanageable and it is only by focusing on a small number of carefully selected options that you can begin to make progress.

Before turning to decision making, it is important to dispel the notion that you can come up with a totally risk-free decision. It is virtually impossible to arrive at a decision which will give you a perfect job in terms of interest, life-style and remuneration. All jobs have their 'price tags' and compromises have to be made in one or other aspect of the total package. Some examples are given below.

Example 1

Stephen has had a very successful academic record from school right through to a post-doctoral fellowship. He wants an occupation which will fully stretch his intellect and produce constant challenges for his analytical problem-solving abilities. Ideally, he would like a job which would reward him well financially in relation to the effort which he puts into it.

One important consideration is the fact that Stephen has a paraplegic child, whose care requires the efforts of both parents working as a team. It would therefore be difficult if Stephen had a job which took him away from home for long spells or required the family to re-locate frequently.

Based on all these factors, Stephen might come up with an evaluation of suitability of two occupations as illustrated in Figure 6.1.

It is up to Stephen to draw his own conclusions from the evaluation, but the graphs highlight a number of thinking points, the answers to which will determine his decision.

- Management consultancy would certainly provide intellectual stimulus, but it would probably not be directly in the field of his current research.
    How important is it to him to continue within his specific discipline?
    Has he exhausted his interest in his current topic of research and might he derive more intellectual satisfaction from tackling something new?

University lecturing	Suitability	
	Low	High
Intellectual stimulus	· ·. · · ·. ·	
Salary	· · · · · · · · · · · · · · ·	
Life style	· · · · · · · · · · · · · · · · · · · ·. · · ·. ·	

Management consultancy	Suitability	
	Low	High
Intellectual stimulus	· ·. · · ·. ·	
Salary	· ·. · · ·. ·	
Life style	· · · · · ·	

Figure 6.1 Comparing occupations (1)

How does he feel about the wider range of interpersonal skills required to cope with workplace situations which might prevent him from concentrating exclusively on mental problem solving?

- As a management consultant he would be less often at home, but on an enhanced salary he could afford to employ care staff for his son.

    How would this alter family relationships?

    Would Stephen miss the experience of caring in person for his son?

Whatever he decides, there will be a 'price-tag', and only Stephen can decide what that should be.

Example 2

Beverley has combined social science research with active involvement in several human rights pressure groups. Many of her friends are people she has met through these campaigning activities. Given her strongly held principles, Beverley would be very wary about joining an organisation of whose investment and equal opportunities policies she did not approve.

She is also concerned not to compromise what she sees as her own identity. Friends' teasing remarks about her having to 'become a suit' in order to get ahead in her career have troubled her more than she cares to admit.

As a result of these concerns Beverley's evaluation of two occupations might be along the lines shown in Figure 6.2.

As with Stephen, Beverley has to think through the issues raised by the graphs.

- As a public affairs officer in a multi-national company might she be able to

Campaign manager, voluntary sector	Suitability	
	Low	High
Interest of job	· ·. · · ·.	
Salary	· · · · · ·	
Life style	· ·. · · ·.	
Identification with employer	· ·. · · ·.	

Public affairs office, multi-national company	Suitability	
	Low	High
Interest of job	· · · · · · · · · · · · · · · · · · ·	
Salary	· ·. · ·.	
Life style	· · · · ·	
Identification with employer	· · · · ·	

Figure 6.2 Comparing occupations (2)

influence policy and direct sponsorship funding in support of the causes in which she believes?

- Is the salary which she could expect to earn in the voluntary sector adequate to meet even very modest commitments?
- How does she feel about the job insecurity usually associated with the voluntary sector?
- Are folk who work in multi-nationals really all 'power dressers'?

Maybe Beverley can draw upon some of the information she has gathered and contacts that she has made in her career search before arriving at her final decision on which path to pursue.

Decision making model

In chapter 2 you saw how career choice is influenced by many internal and external factors. Now that you know how to make a valid self-assessment and how to gather careers information, you can look at a framework for making a decision on your future career path.

The examples of Stephen and Beverley give you an idea of how individuals arrive at decisions on career choices:

Stage 1 They identify factors which are important to them in their career.

Stage 2 They consider various occupations in relation to these factors and check out how good a match there is between what they want and what these occupations require.

Stage 3   They think through any key issues which have come to light as a result of the matching process.

Stage 4   They decide upon the 'best fit', being fully aware of any 'price tag' which they are accepting when deciding on a particular occupation.

The remainder of this chapter allows you to follow this process using the exercises you completed in chapter three and arrive at a decision on your best career options.

Stage 1

Identifying important factors in career choice

In Exercise 6.1, write in the left hand column all the significant factors in your career choice. These might include the following elements:

- skills which you want to use in your work (e.g. problem solving ability; scientific techniques)
- interests which you want to incorporate in the job (e.g. environmental issues, creative design)
- values which are important to you (e.g. serving the community, professional status)
- temperamental considerations (e.g. extrovert/introvert role, degree of autonomy)
- personal circumstances (e.g. location, financial implications)

Exercise 6.1 Self/job matching

My criteria	1	2	3

Stage 2

Comparison of occupations

Once you have entered your criteria in the diagram, select three occupations which you are considering and enter them in the remaining three columns. Now consider each one in turn in relation to your own criteria. Devise your own rating system to indicate how close a match there is between your criteria and the features of the occupation, for instance, three stars or ticks where there is a close match and none at all if there is a wide variance.

In doing this you may discover that on some points you do not have the necessary information to give an accurate rating. Note these and return to the information gathering process described in chapter 5.

When you have filled in all the sections in the diagram, total your scores at the bottom of the chart. Theoretically, your decision should rest with the occupation which has scored the highest mark on your rating system. Sometimes, however, you may look at the raw score and instantly feel a desire to dispute it because you feel more attracted by some of the other occupations. This is a very valuable discovery, as you will find out in the next stage.

Stage 3

Thinking through key issues

The reason why there may be a mismatch between your actual scores and your instinctive reaction is that not all of the factors which you identified in your list of criteria carry an equal weighting. If you have had this reaction, go back over your criteria one by one to identify those which are more important to you than some of the others. You will almost certainly find for those criteria that the occupation you feel instinctively drawn to has scored a high rating. If that is not the case, ask yourself if you have been totally frank about the significance of these criteria.

For example, if you are very keen to be on the cutting edge of scientific discovery, the fact that another job which does not give you that satisfaction but offers a much higher salary may not be at all significant.

Equally, if you have put down location as a prime consideration because of your personal circumstances, but feel pangs of regret when you see that this rules out an occupation which attracts you on other counts, then there is a personal issue involving these constraints which you have to resolve before coming back to a logical process of making a decision on a career.

You have seen what the thinking points were for Stephen and Beverley, but only you can say what the key issues are for you. Keeping in mind your feelings when looking at your completed decision making chart, write in Exercise 6.2 the important issues which you need to consider, and any action which you may require to take. This may include finding out further information (e.g. whether you could afford to take a drop in income while re-training) or discussing personal issues with people on whom they have an impact.

Exercise 6.2 Important considerations

Thinking points	Action required

Stage 4

Making a decision

Once you have thought through the issues which arose in stage 3, adjust the scores in your diagram to reflect your final decision. So that you are fully aware of the consequences of your decision, rank your choices in order in Exercise 6.3, and alongside them put your estimation of the 'price tag' of each option (see the example above the exercise).

Living with your decision

Once you have completed the decision making process, you are ready to move on to finding vacancies and making applications. Part IV of this book will help you through those stages. Before leaving this chapter on decision making, however, it is important to address the concerns of readers who may feel quite anxious about making a decision in case they make the wrong choice.

First, accept the fact that no human being is gifted with perfect, infallible insight in all circumstances. Mistakes and wrong choices do happen, but in the case of career planning these are rarely irreversible – and virtually every job brings benefits from experience which can be woven into the picture of what you have to offer your next employer – even if that is a more determined conviction to make your career in an area other than your present occupation.

Second, be aware that as life circumstances change, so too do our needs and aspirations in relation to our career. The decision which you make now may be logical and appropriate for this stage in your life, but it may need to be reviewed

Exercise 6.3 Example

Choice	Price tag
Civil Service research	Relocation necessary
Academic librarian	Training required

Exercise 6.3 Weighing the consequences of decisions

Choice	Price tag
1	
2	
3	

two years from now if you find yourself in a different situation. Indeed, it is wise to do a stock-taking on the aptness of your career every so often.

Remember that not every career decision has to be governed totally by logic. Speaking about the stages in a process makes everything sound very mechanistic, but as you have seen there is plenty of scope for assessing your feelings and incorporating your instincts into the weighting which you give to the factors which have a bearing on your career decision. At the end of the day, strong instincts are usually correct.

Finally, it is impossible to remove all risks from decision making. Life itself is a risky business, and any action which leads to change involves a leap of faith. Take courage from the fact that some of the most successful and satisfied people entered their careers though what appears to be serendipity. Having said that, sensible sky-divers have always double-checked their equipment and so the time which you are spending now on working through the process of career choice will help to assure you that you are well equipped to jump in the right direction.

Part III

Focus on career routes

Chapter 7

Routes to an academic career

If you are seeking an academic post – in either lecturing or research – you are placing yourself in a very competitive market. In this respect, it is no different from hundreds of other areas which you might choose to enter. The same rules apply as for any other competitive field:

Find out exactly what selectors are looking for and give them plenty of evidence that you can meet their requirements.

For an academic post, subject knowledge is clearly of paramount importance. For instance, a specialist in medieval French poetry will not be appointed to a post requiring in-depth knowledge of contemporary French novels. None the less, it cannot be assumed that subject knowledge alone will win the day. Many other factors are now taken into account when making academic appointments. This chapter outlines areas in which it would be useful to gain experience, as well as issues of which it would be wise to be aware. First of all, however, it may be useful to look at some typical routes into academic posts (Figures 7.1 and 7.2).

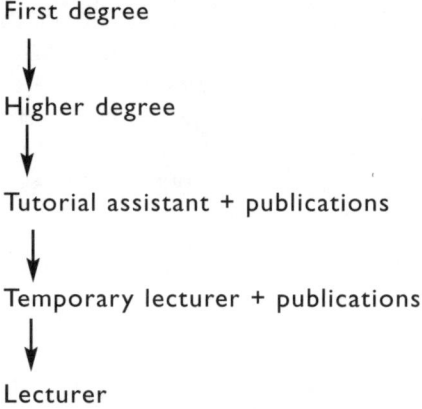

First degree

↓

Higher degree

↓

Tutorial assistant + publications

↓

Temporary lecturer + publications

↓

Lecturer

Figure 7.1 Route to lecturing

First degree

↓

Higher degree

↓

Post-doctoral fellowship + publications

↓

Research assistant + publications

↓

Research officer + publications

↓

Senior research officer

Figure 7.2 Route to a senior research post

When described in a linear flow chart, these routes seem very obvious, but the charts do not take account of the time required to move through these stages. Many people become discouraged at an intermediate point in the process when all that they can find is temporary work. None the less, the charts are valid as a description of the route to follow. It would be unlikely today for anyone finishing a higher degree to step immediately into a permanent lecturing or research post, unless they had considerable relevant experience prior to completing a higher degree.

There may, of course, be diversions on the route, for instance spending time in industry, commerce or public service could be a useful addition to an individual's experience before pursuing an academic career, which would benefit from such first hand exposure to practical work. Such experience could provide routes which might look something like the examples given in Figures 7.3. and 7.4.

It is clear from all of the sample routes given in Figures 7.3 and 7.4 that a candidate for an academic lecturing or research post must gather together a portfolio consisting of both qualifications and relevant experience in order to be competitive, and ultimately, successful. The next section summarises the components which it would be useful to have in your portfolio.

Valuable assets for your portfolio

Qualifications

For a long term career in either lecturing or research, higher degree qualifications of some kind are becoming almost obligatory. The level at which these are attained, however, is variable from one field to another. For instance, in areas

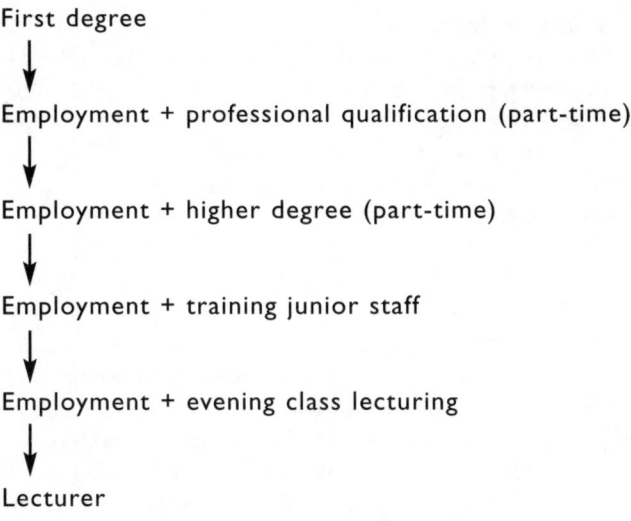

First degree

↓

Employment + professional qualification (part-time)

↓

Employment + higher degree (part-time)

↓

Employment + training junior staff

↓

Employment + evening class lecturing

↓

Lecturer

Figure 7.3 Alternative route to lecturing

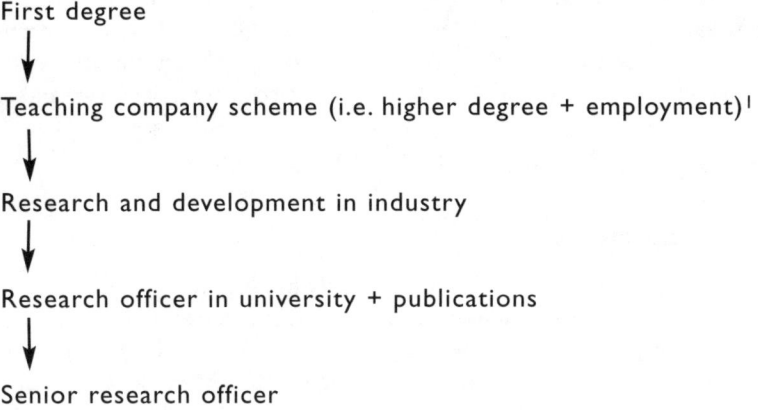

First degree

↓

Teaching company scheme (i.e. higher degree + employment)[1]

↓

Research and development in industry

↓

Research officer in university + publications

↓

Senior research officer

Figure 7.4 Alternative route to a senior research post

such as chemistry and bioscience, where relatively high proportions of graduates go on to take higher degrees, a Ph.D. may be considered essential for posts of even modest seniority. Likewise, in the arts and humanities where funding for posts may be difficult to obtain, a Ph.D. may be the requirement. Conversely, in fields such as business, education and engineering more stress may be laid on having appropriate work experience outside higher education and a Master's level degree may be considered adequate.

There are possible entry points to temporary posts at the bottom of the ladder for those who are still in the process of studying for a higher degree. Graduates with a good first degree (preferably first class, but possibly an upper second) may find full or part-time work on temporary contracts as tutorial assistants, demonstrators, research assistants or lecturers in continuing education departments. Any of these opportunities provides a valuable foundation on which to build a portfolio of relevant experience.

Publications

For both lecturers and researchers, publications are a convenient measure by which selectors can gauge active participation in scholarship. Judgement is based not only on the number of publications which a scholar has, but also on the journals in which they were published and the standing of the collaborators within their academic discipline. Thus, it may be of more benefit to be third in a list of authors where the chief author is an eminent authority in the subject, and the journal is well-known and a frequent source of citations, than it would be to appear as a sole author of a very slender article in a little-known publication.

Having articles accepted for publication in a well-respected journal can be an uphill struggle, especially if you are an unknown quantity to the editors. It is therefore useful to seek advice from a supervisor or mentor in your department as to how to break through into print. It is more than likely that the best first step is to seek to be cited as a co-author of an article from a departmental group of collaborators. If, however, after six years you are still appearing as a tenth author in a list, your strategy will need to be re-thought!

Research and project funding

All universities depend on attracting research funding from research councils, Government departments, industry and commerce, medical and other charities, and overseas clients. This explains why so many posts are on short-term contracts as the money is in relation to research projects with set timescales. Since such contracts are vital to a university's finances, a successful track record in securing funding is an added recommendation of a candidate for an academic post.

In the past, regulations applied by some research councils and universities imposed tight constraints on those researchers who were eligible to apply for funding, effectively restricting this to principal investigators and excluding research assistants, even though the funding proposal may have arisen directly out of their work. Since the appearance of the Concordat and Codes of Practice for Research Staff in most universities, this problem is being addressed, and it has become easier for researchers on lower grades to put forward funding proposals if countersigned by senior staff.

Even so, it is not easy to succeed in bids for funding. Currently the Biotechnology and Biological Sciences Research Council manages to fund fewer than one in five of all bids received, while the Economic and Social Science Research Council can fund only one-third of all projects which are rated grade A. Despite the odds, however, it is essential to gain experience of making bids as this method of funding higher education research is likely to continue.

For those in the early part of their academic career, it would be useful to look at successful (or even unsuccessful A rated) bids and have a supervisor or mentor explain how they were put together and the sources of information used. In demonstrating their future potential as successful bidders for funding, inexperienced researchers can point to any scholarships or fellowships which they have won in a competitive process and any other activities which have involved a negotiation process, for example, bidding as an executive officer of a university society for funding from a central source or an external sponsor.

Project management

If an institution gains a reputation for failing to finish projects on time and over-spending on the budget, this can be fatal to its prospects of securing further funding. It is important, therefore, that selectors should try to ensure that new staff can deliver the outcomes of projects within budget and by the agreed deadline. Candidates therefore should provide evidence of their ability to meet this criterion, primarily within the academic context, but from other fields as well.

There are numerous reasons why projects go wrong, and the more people who are involved in them, the greater the potential risk of delay. If you know that projects in which you have been involved have fallen behind schedule, be ready with a clear explanation of what caused this, what was done to retrieve the situation and what you learned from the process. As an experienced project manager has said, 'It is not necessarily a crime to be running late, but it is always a crime not to know that you are running late'.[2]

Teaching experience

For lecturing posts it is obviously desirable to have gained any kind of teaching experience in the higher education sector. Practices in making this kind of experience available to postgraduate research students and research assistants vary widely from department to department. In some this is discouraged while in others it is virtually a requirement. If your aspirations lie in this direction, it is worth discussing with a supervisor or mentor in your department what the opportunities are within the department for individual or group tutorial work, demonstrating, marking exam scripts or lecturing on a module close to your research topic.

Further options exist outside your department through Continuing Education Departments, which now accredit many of their courses. You may also find teaching opportunities in evening classes on relevant subjects in a local further education college, which may have the benefit of bringing you into contact with practitioners who are seeking a theoretical under-pinning for their day to day work.

Many institutions now offer training courses in teaching and learning methods for teaching assistants. Take advantage of any such courses, some of which may lead to a certificate of the University, a NVQ/SVQ award or a qualification of the Institute of Teaching and Learning. A course will introduce you to current theories of teaching and learning which you may be expected to be aware of at an interview for a lecturing post. For further background reading on such issues, contact the learning support centre or staff development unit in your university, which may hold resources on these topics.

Quality assessment

In recent years there has been a greatly increased emphasis in universities on accountability and quality assessment. All kinds of funding bodies wish to be assured that they are receiving value for money and that universities are self-regulating on quality issues.

Two of the most significant exercises in this respect are quality audit of teaching and research assessment. During your time in a department it is likely that it will be preparing for, going through or drawing learning points from one or other of these exercises. Reports by the funding councils on these assessments are made available to the public and are usually on open access in university libraries. If you have not been directly involved in meeting assessors or completing forms on your research activities, at least you can familiarise yourself with the format of the reports and the assessors' criteria in order to understand what they consider important. Better still, ask someone in your department who was deeply involved in the process to talk to you about how the department conducted its self-assessment and what new procedures or codes of practice it put in place in order to meet the assessors' criteria.

Understanding higher education issues

It is helpful for your future prospects in academia if you are alert to major issues within higher education. For instance, how much do you know about the following topics?

- the impact of higher student numbers on teaching methods in higher education
- accreditation of prior learning in lieu of formal academic entry qualifications
- costing of overheads in research funding bids
- innovative applications of information technology in student centred learning
- scope for collaboration between higher education and industry in your field of research.

First of all, you need to find out which specific issues are liable to be important to the department or the unit which you hope to join. This is where discussion with an experienced lecturer or researcher can brief you on topics likely to come up at an interview. Other useful sources of information are listed below and you should use as many of them as you can to keep yourself well informed.

- departmental staff meetings
- minutes of Faculty or Senate meetings (often lodged in a university library)
- *The Times Higher Education Supplement* (also available via the Internet)
- newsletters of the Committee of Vice-Chancellors and Principals
- newsletters of the funding councils
- circulars and newsletters of appropriate unions (e.g. Association of University Teachers, National Association of Teachers in Further and Higher Education).

Networking

Alongside these measures, it is essential that you develop a network of contacts. While permanent academic posts are usually advertised externally, many temporary posts may be initially advertised only internally, and often at short notice if funding has been delayed and grant-holders are eager to make an early start on a project. It is therefore important that you should be connected to the grapevine on which such posts are advertised.

Networking can be an important route into any profession, but it is worth mentioning here what this means in the academic context. In the first instance, who are your contacts? These consist of anyone with an interest in your field of study: your research supervisor, co-researchers, guest lecturers, people whom you meet at conferences and authors of publications allied to your field. Some departments and institutions have a formal mentoring scheme for junior staff, or occasionally for all staff. Where this exists, it often has as one of its purposes an intention to help staff with their career advancement by advising them on what is required for career progression. Whether or not such a scheme exists in your institution, it is a good idea to find someone who will act informally in the capacity of a mentor, someone who can help you to make sense of the labyrinth of university departmental and faculty administration and point out who are the most useful and influential contacts in your institution.

The role of conferences in academia is central to becoming visible within your discipline. As a participant at conferences you will not only become aware of current developments, debates and controversies in your field of research, but also meet face to face people who may potentially become research collaborators, external examiners or reviewers, or your interviewers in a future selection panel. If you progress to giving papers at conferences, not only will you become better known within your discipline, but you will potentially have material for a publication. Even if the conference programme is disappointing, the contacts which are developed at such events can be very beneficial for your future personal and professional development, as well as boosting your morale.

Since networking comes more easily to some people than to others, it is necessary to dispel some misapprehensions about what networking means. It certainly does not mean boring people with your job search at every possible opportunity. What it does mean is sharing information which is of common interest, in other words, giving as well as receiving. Amongst the information which you will give is notification of your availability for employment now or in the future. In addition to an exchange of knowledge and expertise, you may wish to seek advice on how to improve your employment prospects, how to conduct your job search and details of any vacancies known to your contacts, either in their own institutions or elsewhere. Amongst these contacts may be people who can help you with one of the most crucial factors in academic selection, knowing what the selectors want.

Selection criteria of higher education selectors

The assets listed above are closely related to the selection criteria used by academic selectors when drawing up a short list and interviewing candidates for posts. You will be better able to prepare your written documentation and your interview strategy if you understand the process adopted by selectors and the criteria which they set.

Following preparation of a job description selectors usually draw up a list of essential and desirable criteria for the post. This is known as a person specification. An example of such a selection tool is shown in Figure 7.5.

The rigour with which the person specification is applied depends on the size and quality of the field of candidates. It would be unusual to select a candidate who does not meet all of the essential criteria, but this might happen if there were few applicants and one was strong on all but one of them. If an advertisement has elicited a good response, it is more likely that the desirable criteria will also be brought into play in order to reduce the number of applications to a manageable short-list. As an applicant you cannot know which way the selection will be conducted and so you have to present as much solid evidence as you can of all criteria mentioned or hinted at in an advertisement or a job description.

Details of CVs, applications and interviews for academic posts are included in chapters 10–12. Before leaving the subject of academic posts, however, there are some further issues to consider.

Long term prospects in higher education

The figures quoted in chapter 1 indicate that there are far more people in temporary contracts than will ever find permanent posts in higher education. That need not necessarily deter you from setting off down an
acade

JOB TITLE
DEPARTMENT

I	Educational/Professional Qualifications
	Essential
	Desirable

2	Previous Experience/Training
	Essential
	Desirable

3	Job-related Skills and Achievements
	Essential
	Desirable

4	Personal Qualities and Abilities
	Essential
	Desirable

5	Other Factors (e.g. presentation skills, research abilities)
	Essential
	Desirable

Figure 7.5 Sample person specification
Reproduced by kind permission of the University of Strathclyde,
Director of Personnel

- Prospects are variable from one discipline to another. You may be fortunate to be in a discipline where the competition for longer term contracts or permanent tenure is less severe than average, but you need to investigate the situation.
- It rarely looks bad to have a spell of employment in a university on your CV. Even if you switch track later, many employers will assume a high level of intelligence plus good analytical and research skills on the basis of your university experience. If you leave it for a long time before changing direction, however, some employers may be sceptical about your ability to adapt to a very different working environment.
- If the most important factor for you in employment is the opportunity to work very closely within your academic specialisation as opposed to using transferable skills in a different context, an academic career offers you the best opportunity to do so. This may override the disadvantages of lack of secure employment and relatively low wages in the early part of your career.

Even if you weather the uncertainty of initial short term contracts and win through to a permanent appointment, you may find that over a lifetime people who graduated with you and entered other professions may have achieved higher earnings and more fringe benefits. On the other hand, university staff are not on the lowest rung of the salary ladder in relation to the full range of professions. Those who are on longer term or permanent contracts are on incremental scales, unlike many graduates in industry who may have to negotiate every pay rise.

If the pace of progress and the level of remuneration in the UK seem unsatisfactory, you may wish to use your experience of higher education in the UK as a springboard to a teaching or research post in a university overseas. The geographic areas in which higher education is burgeoning most rapidly are the Middle East and South-East Asia. Depending on your speciality, there may be options elsewhere, either on an exchange basis or on a straight contract if visa problems can be overcome. A spell of teaching overseas may well be attractive to UK universities with a large population of overseas students at a later point in your career.

Gender issues

Theoretically, there are no obstacles preventing women from reaching the highest levels of an academic career. Indeed, some aspects of academic life are very suitable for women. For instance, promotion is primarily on merit, based on academic achievements. Job-sharing and part-time working are fairly common and there are often crèche facilities on campus.

Why then is it that the distribution of women in higher education shows a pattern similar to that in several other professions, with women over-represented in the lowest grades in both teaching and research, but scarcely visible in the ranks of the professoriate and senior management? (See Table 1.4.)

Part of the problem is that fewer permanent posts are becoming available and women are over-represented in short-term contract posts, few of which are on senior grades. There is also the issue of your success being measured by the number of your publications. Women who have had a career break have often a gap in their publications record, which counts against them. Women also tend to be less visible in the committees and governing bodies of universities, such as Court and Senate, and therefore often have a lower profile on campus.

These are generalisations and there are, of course, exceptions. Recently, however, some positive steps have been taken to encourage wider participation in university life and so to improve women's career prospects in higher education.

- The CVCP has established a Commission on University Career Opportunities (CUCO) to monitor and promote equal opportunities in university career structures.
- The Concordat lays down improved conditions for maternity leave during a short term contract.
- The Engineering and Physical Sciences Research Council has made part-time research fellowships available, which are particularly suitable for researchers with family commitments.
- The Committee of Scottish Higher Education Principals runs courses on Managing Personal and Professional Development for women in research, teaching, administration and support services.

These measures and the adoption and monitoring of equal opportunities policies in universities should lead to a gradual increase in the number of positive role models for women in higher education.

Staff with disabilities

Because people with disabilities are under-represented among the student population at tertiary level, there is a subsequent under-representation amongst university staff as insufficient numbers of people with disabilities have appropriate qualifications. As more people with special needs come through university, this situation should alter.

On the whole universities tend to be less well adapted than schools to the access and special equipment needs of people with disabilities. The Disability Discrimination Act (1996) has spelled out certain obligations of universities in respect of such provision, but practical financial constraints have often hindered access improvement schemes.

Once access and equipment issues are resolved, universities are otherwise a good environment for graduates with disabilities. Advancement is on the basis of intellect rather than physical or sensory ability. Most posts do not require great mobility and a regular work place can be adapted to the requirements of an individual. On the whole, staff are supportive of the practical needs of colleagues without making fuss. Above all, in higher education people with disabilities are much less likely to encounter the infuriating stereotypical assumption that a physical or sensory impairment has an implication of a lack of mental ability and so they can be much freer to reach their full potential in an academic environment.

International scholars

Students from overseas are disproportionately represented at postgraduate level. It is only natural that many of them want to stay and develop their research further via a post-doctoral fellowship or a research assistant post.

Where students are members of European Union countries or are in other exempt categories, there is no work permit problem if they find a suitable post. If, however, they are in the UK on a student visa and require a work permit in order to move to a different status, a university wishing to appoint them must apply to the Home Office, stating a case as to why a permit should be granted. In very specialised areas of research it may well be possible to argue that an individual has unique knowledge and that a post could not be filled by a UK or EU national.

Summary

Research councils and university managers agreed in the Concordat that a permanent career in academic research is likely to be achieved by only a minority of the very best researchers. With the awarding of more and more short-term contracts, it is also becoming more difficult to secure a tenured lecturing post. Nonetheless, for those whose commitment is equal to their talent, it is possible to achieve an academic career, whether that be composed of a series of temporary contracts or a permanent post.

This chapter has summarised the additional factors which can tip the balance among candidates of equal academic merit, namely:

- acquiring publications in well recognised journals with collaborators who are frequently cited
- gaining experience of applying for and securing research funding
- demonstrating efficient project management which consistently delivers stated outcomes on time and within budget
- gaining experience of designing, delivering and evaluating degree level courses
- understanding the process of quality assessment in teaching and research
- being conversant with current issues in higher education
- networking with people who are aware of your ambitions and can advise on your job search strategy
- using conferences as a way of raising your profile within your discipline and as a possible springboard for publications
- analysing the selection criteria of academic selectors and providing convincing evidence that you meet their standards.

After you have done all of these things, you may discover that 'luck occurs where preparation meets opportunity'!

Case studies

The following case studies, which are based on real people although names have been changed, show how three individuals achieved long-term careers in lecturing and research posts in higher education. Their frank comments indicate both the plus and minus points of an academic career.

Cheryl Wilson

Background

'On finishing school in Lancashire, I went to a Scottish university, where I gained a 2.1 honours degree in pharmacology. By this stage I had developed a strong interest in cardiovascular pharmacology and I spent the next three years completing a Ph.D. in this subject with researchers with an international reputation in this subject. I found this very exhilarating.

'As my postgraduate studies neared completion, I debated whether to pursue a career in industry or to aim for a postdoctoral post. My decision to choose academic work was based largely on a preference for academic freedom to pursue lines of research which interested me. Another reason for choosing academia was that I genuinely wanted to teach at higher education level – unlike some of my contemporaries who regarded teaching as a necessary evil to hold down their research posts.

'Following four years as a postdoctoral research fellow in the university where I took my Ph.D., I secured a post as a research lecturer in a department of physiology and pharmacology, helped, I think, by the prestige of being one of the winners of the Young Investigators Award of the European Society of Cardiology. Ten years after completing my Ph.D. I was appointed senior lecturer and I'm still in that post, having sustained my research interests during two brief spells of maternity leave.'

Work as an academic

'I always seem to be working on umpteen fronts simultaneously – and that's not counting the home front! Bidding for research grants and ensuring delivery of high quality research within tight deadlines are a constant feature of the job. In fourteen years, I have secured twenty-seven grants amounting to hundreds of thousands of pounds. Securing the larger grants is dependent on having a good research team, establishing credibility in the academic community through sound publications and visibility at conferences and in learned societies as well as assessing correctly the research councils' funding preferences.

'In my field it is also important to maintain good links with the pharmaceutical companies which fund much of the research. Some of the valuable research visits which I have undertaken in the UK, Germany and Hungary to industrial and university research centres have been funded by industrial and Government sponsors.

'As well as undertaking research, it is essential to find time to write it up for publications. I now have a long list of publications in mainstream professional journals. This has resulted in invitations to speak at conferences and to join the editorial board of the *British Journal of Pharmacology*. Acting as a referee for papers submitted to journals is another time-consuming activity, but it is an essential step towards being recognised in my field.

'I have also been Honorary Treasurer for a national research society for three years. This involves a great deal of work, but it brings the benefit of building up research collaborations through new contacts.

'All of this research related work is in addition to lectures, laboratory classes, small group teaching, one to one tutorials, student presentations and supervision of postgraduates. I try to be an innovative teacher and have enjoyed collaborating with colleagues to develop a new method of team working for final year practical classes. It was really satisfying when an educational methods article on this innovation received a commendation in a national competition.

'The list of responsibilities does not end with teaching commitments. Faculty committees are a good way of being visible – although they have the disadvantage of usually being rather boring! If you want to be visible – organise a conference! It will send you out of your mind with worry, but if you make a good job of it, both the scientific community and the University will sit up and take notice.

'On a wider front I feel highly committed to encouraging other women to succeed in academia and so I devote a few days per year to acting as a trainer on courses for both senior women and those on temporary contracts in universities.'

Pros and cons of academic life

'There is still some degree of academic freedom in higher education, though possibly less so than when I became a post-doctoral fellow fourteen years ago. I find my work extremely stimulating and highly rewarding – especially research collaborations. I enjoy all the aspects of my work which involve people. My favourite day of the year is meeting up with all the mums and dads on graduation day.

'Although working hours are very long, they can be quite flexible outside class times. To that extent I consider academic life a good working environment for anyone who wants to combine a career and a family.

'It has to be said that academic pay rates do not compare with those of industrial counterparts in my field. Competition for funding has become much more intense over the last few years and there is always the anxiety of wondering whether projects will be able to proceed if the latest bid is not successful. The need to keep winning funds spurs me on in all my other activities because they all contribute to the kind of profile which leads to success.'

Factors leading to success

'I'm sure that my progress has been helped by the fact that at an early stage in my career I realised the value of collaborative networking, not only within professional circles, but also across the University community at Faculty level and through an inter-disciplinary staff development group. This visibility is necessary alongside a sound academic performance to gain research grants and securing publication of research. In the academic world, as in any other context, she who sits in a corner, quietly getting on with her work, will be allowed to sit there . . . until her contract expires! In order to have allies, you have to be known.'

Messages from Cheryl

'To succeed in academia, you have to really want to do the job. We certainly are not in it for the money – and at times it can drive you demented when you realise what vast amounts of work you have undertaken within ridiculous time-scales.

'Nevertheless, when I think of the diversity of what I do in an average week, let alone a year, and virtually all of it work which I enjoy doing, I wouldn't swap this for any other career. If you are fascinated by your research subject and want to go on exploring it, while also sharing your enthusiasm for it with the next generation of students, it is worth all the hard work in order to have that opportunity.

'The fact that we now have to adopt a more business-like approach to finding funding for our research is inevitable in today's world. I don't know research scientists in industry today who are having money poured into their research without accountability. Having seen both sectors, I'm content to stay in higher education where I have the extra bonuses of student contact and opportunities for publication.'

Stephen Cameron

Background

'I left school after fifth year and went straight into a B.Sc. degree course in geography at my local university. On graduating with a first class honours degree, I obtained an ESRC Doctorate studentship and immediately started Ph.D. research. After that I accepted a six months research assistant post, which eventually led to a nine month teaching fellowship. One year later, I gained a lectureship in geography in a small department in another university and have remained there for five years.

'I suppose I've been lucky as that smooth succession may not be the norm. On the other hand, I have passed through the system with little work experience outside academia. Looking back, I cannot remember ever taking a conscious decision that this was what I wanted to do with my life. Indeed, if anything, I entered under the supposition that I would do it for a couple of years and then move on. I now find that getting out is not easy and that a narrow academic background is not exactly what employers want.'

Work as an academic

'My department is being subjected to the same kinds of pressures as many other departments in Britain. I spend over a hundred hours a year in lecture contact, and many more again in tutorial support work. I teach across all years and supervise both Masters and Ph.D. students. As the department is small, I have a number of major administration duties, including being a year co-ordinator, being in charge of postgraduate student recruitment, monitoring and supervision and being responsible for student careers development within the department. I find these jobs wholly overwhelming at times and it is impossible to do them to the level they deserve. The consequence is that jobs have to be prioritised, but there is always the feeling of never doing them true justice.

'No matter how great these pressures are, they are dwarfed by the pressures to produce research output for the research assessment exercise. Research is without question the number one emphasis within the department and as a consequence it has proved to be the source of greatest stress. I spend two to three hours four nights a week on research, and all day Sunday. Research is also the source of most conflict within the department and shapes attitudes and relationships fundamentally.'

Pros and cons of academic life

'The consequence of fierce research pressures and very heavy teaching and administration loads has been that I have been forced to withdraw from interaction within the department and work more at an individual level. The days of long summers and unstructured weeks feeding into the generation of a climate of learning and a good sense of community among students are gone. The primary concern is the retention of a viable CV in an academic climate which calls for very strict time management and therefore a reduction in student contact. It is a position which I find hard to reconcile at times and has led to periodic disillusionment with what I am doing. So far, however, it has not dented my enjoyment of the job and of undertaking teaching and administration to the point at which I would wish to leave academic life. Fortunately, there are now excellent support networks in universities in both the research and teaching fronts, and my continuing enthusiasm is due to the fact that I feel my competence in both spheres expanding through regular contact with these networks.'

Factors leading to success

'I suppose that my success to date can be attributed to a good academic performance, plus a willingness to work a seventy hour week and to volunteer for a very wide range of teaching and administrative responsiblities. Having committed myself to doing these tasks, I try to ensure that they are done well. I guess I have built up a reputation in the department as a sound performer who can be relied upon to deliver competent research, teaching and administration.'

Messages from Stephen

'In my opinion, university life is just as fast and hard as that experienced in the crazy world of the stock exchange. Academics are expected to produce international class research, to teach to ever larger classes, to assume highly responsible administration roles and to do all of this within very tight time constraints. Performance is constantly measured and in a small department there is great pressure to assume more work in teaching and administration than can be achieved even within very long working hours. This results in the feeling that you are not doing all these tasks to a satisfactory level.

'This is not the world of the perfectionist. Organisation skills, a preparedness to work long hours, and a research active mind are now the key qualities. Interest in student affairs, being a dynamic lecturer, and poring over the heady details of esoteric academic texts take second place to the pressure to churn out good research. In the present climate, survival in academia depends upon accepting this balance of priorities.'

Katherine Scott

Background

'I fell into research by accident. I am a classic Scottish working class kid. I could draw reasonably well and so went to art school. After completing three years of a four year course, I dropped out. Through working in a hospital vacation job I realised that what I really wanted to do was work with people, maybe as an art therapist or social worker.

'Once I ceased to be a student and started to pay income tax, I realised that I was very badly paid at the hospital and couldn't maintain even my modest lifestyle. The only organisation which thought anything of my qualifications was the Civil Service. I went along to the Civil Service Commission, had a good interview, and they sent me to the Commission on Industrial Relations (CIR) as a clerical officer, because I'd said I was "interested in people". The CIR was a great organisation. It was also understaffed. Because I was keen and articulate I was co-opted to help with non-clerical officer tasks – administering attitude surveys, helping with earnings surveys – by the end carrying out case studies of organisations on my own. I loved it.

'I embarked on 'A' levels in sociology and English literature at evening classes. I realised quite soon that I got a real kick out of the academic side of it, and applied to London University to do a degree in sociology instead. I got 'A' levels after one year of evening classes, so the next step was a place at London University, to do a sociology degree. I enjoyed the course and did well enough to be accepted to do an MA and be offered a research assistant post at a polytechnic.'

Work as an academic

'Since then in my career I've largely been a camp follower who moved with my husband and family but I have somehow always continued to research or write and – this is probably the most important bit – stay in the professional networks. When I was doing my Ph.D., my supervisor encouraged me to join the British Sociological Association, which was a lifeline when my kids were small and I was still finishing my Ph.D. When we moved to Oxford mid-Ph.D. friends suggested I would be an ideal editor for *Network*, the BSA newsletter, published three times per annum. This involved keeping abreast with relevant policy and practice, writing about it, persuading others to write news items and commentaries. I loved doing it. It also meant I became an ex-officio member of the BSA Executive Committee and learned useful publishing related skills. This has been important in keeping me informed and motivated.

'As I completed my Ph.D., I secured a post as a research fellow, then senior research fellow at the Institute for Employment Research. I left to teach in a new university for five years in the middle, then returned to be principal research fellow, involved in some fascinating projects en route, all of which benefited from my early experience in the Commission for Industrial Relations. In that role a large proportion of my time is taken up with bids to keep research funding flowing and external relations with bodies which commission research, or might be persuaded to do so!

'Turning out a large volume of high quality academic writing is the main part of the job and I have always enjoyed that. Over the years I have built up a good deal of experience in teaching – from course design to supervision of Ph.D. students – partly because it gives me satisfaction and partly to ensure that I have a well rounded academic profile.

'That balance was an essential prerequisite for my latest move. I have recently been appointed a Professor of Employment Studies in a university which is closer to where my husband works. We are both looking forward to a life minus the long distance commuting which we have both had to do for more years than we care to remember. It hasn't in all honesty, been a planned career – but it does look quite coherent when I look back – at least since the Commission on Industrial Relations experience.'

Pros and cons of academic life

'To some extent we create our own pros and cons in academic life. One thing I care intensely about is doing things as well as possible, which maybe leads to stress and overload sometimes but pleases sponsors. Contract research is highly stimulating and tends to be policy-related – which I like. The down-side is that it is often frantically busy, balancing several projects at a time – and there is never enough time to scan and reflect. I feel strongly that work for contract researchers has intensified within the last few years and competition become more oppressive, as sponsors want research outputs in unrealistically short timescales and are unable or unwilling to pay enough to enable researchers to invest sufficient time and resources to really investigate the issues.'

Messages from Katherine

'The message to readers is that there are always opportunities to build 'atypical' careers if they are prepared to take them – but they probably involve working harder for less money in the short term. I have been 'lucky' in having a breadwinner husband who could support me throughout very low earning voluntary and part-time periods when I was completing my Ph.D. and establishing my reputation as a researcher. However, some of it has been down to having the courage to ask for support in unlikely circumstances. For example, when I took on the *Network* editorship, I arranged to negotiate an office in the Social Studies Building at Oxford University, with a telephone – which gave me professional status and access to colleagues although the *Network* post was strictly unpaid. Through that, I was invited to do (low paid) Oxford University undergraduate tutoring, which added a new dimension to my CV.'

Thinking points

As described by the people in these profiles, academic life is definitely not an easy option, and they all acknowledge that the route into it is becoming more competitive than when they began their careers. They recognise the disadvantages: exceptionally long working hours, relentless pressure to bring in research funding in a climate where excellent research proposals fall by the wayside for lack of resources, and a lengthy period of relatively low pay at the beginning of an academic career. What keeps them motivated is a genuine fascination with their research interests and a pleasure in communicating their knowledge to students and research collaborators.

When deciding whether you want to begin or to continue down the path to an academic career, consider the thinking points raised by these case studies.

Recognise your source of motivation

A large part of job satisfaction comes from having a strong motivation to go to work every day and to enjoy what you do there. For most academics this motivation comes from a life-long enjoyment of their academic discipline and from working in a culture in which intellectual excellence is respected.

What do you consider to be your main motivator?

- Is your interest in your subject wearing thin, or do you feel stimulated to delve ever deeper into your research topic?
- Is your interest in your academic discipline sufficient to offset potential disadvantages such as the insecurity of short term contracts and relatively low pay?

Extend your portfolio of accomplishments

All of the people in the case studies recognise that it is not sufficient to do good research and expect to be successful as a result. They are aware of the need to volunteer to undertake other commitments in the form of teaching, administrative tasks, voluntary work for professional bodies and collaborative activities in their university and professional communities.

- How are you working currently to expand your range of activities beyond your immediate field of research or job description?
- If that seems impossible, how can you streamline what you are doing currently in order to fit in at least one of the additional activities which are necessary for a successful academic career?
- How can you play to your strengths by volunteering to do something which you will enjoy as well as enhancing your track record as a highly competent performer in more than one dimension?

Increase your visibility

The people in the profiles understand that it is necessary to be seen to be active and successful. This does not mean that they are vain or boastful. They are simply being pragmatic because they know that successful academic careers are built on one's reputation in the academic community.

- Apart from your immediate colleagues, who knows that you exist, within your university and your professional community?
- How do you think that you are regarded, in terms of not only your research output, but also your reputation for collaboration, reliability and organisational ability?
- How could you raise your profile in situations where you can both give and gain, for instance, through conferences, workshops and even social gatherings?

Acknowledge why you stay in academia

Although they describe themselves as having an obvious or an opportunist route into research and academic teaching, all three of the people in the case studies know that there are other career options which they could have followed and they reckon that they are better suited by academic work than they might be in other occupations. Ask yourself on what basis you have arrived at a similar decision, if indeed you have!

- Have you weighed up various career options and concluded that there are more advantages for you in academic work than in other occupations?
- Are you remaining on an academic track because it is familiar or because it is expected of you, or because it uses all your talents in a way which gives you immense satisfaction?
- How important is the academic environment to you? Does it stimulate you to do your best work – or does it place any constraints on your development to your maximum potential?

There are no right or wrong answers to these questions, only answers which are right for you at this time and stage in your career and your life. Whatever you do, it is best if you have chosen to do it for positive reasons rather than by default. Before making a decision, you may like to find out about routes to alternative careers which other researchers have taken. You can do so in the next chapter.

Chapter 8

Routes to other careers

Once you begin to look beyond academic careers, the scope is almost endless. The PROSPECT (HE) computer aided guidance system holds details of approximately 400 occupations suitable for graduates, but that is the tip of a very large iceberg. New occupations are constantly being created. For example, web master and call centre manager are occupations which did not exist five years ago. Many people have occupations which defy classification under traditional job titles, while others have developed 'portfolio careers', doing two or three or even more jobs alongside one another, for example, tourist guide and local history lecturer.

As in chapter 4, it is not feasible or sensible to adopt an encyclopaedic approach here, given the enormous range of readers' interests and experience. This chapter therefore concentrates on demonstrating from real case histories how it is possible to develop career routes in a huge variety of directions following a foundation in academic research. The following case studies are based on real people, although names and details have been changed to preserve anonymity. At the end of the chapter the messages from these career changers are drawn together into thinking points which you can apply to your own career planning.

Same discipline, different employer

The people in the first group of case studies have continued in the same field as their academic research, but career progression has been attained through moving to a different employer, and in one case into self-employment.

Margaret Simmons, economic consultant

Background

'When I graduated with a first class honours degree in economics, I had thought about becoming an economic analyst in the finance sector. I hadn't made much progress, however, because following some early rejections after completing difficult application forms I had to decide to concentrate on my studies and leave job seeking until later. When my department offered me a post as a research assistant, it seemed so easy to accept and to stay a little longer in a familiar environment.'

Research experience

'My first post was on a three months' contract and involved a good deal of straightforward number crunching to provide data for a senior researcher. By the time this finished, I had decided to try something more challenging and so I enrolled for a Ph.D. on the evaluation of incentives to women to become self-employed. This involved a good deal of field research, including interviews with entrepreneurs and representatives of funding bodies.'

Transition

'Having spoken to other researchers, I knew that research assistant posts could be more challenging than my first post after graduation, but I had particularly enjoyed the inter-action with people in small businesses. By the end of my Ph.D. studies I was convinced that I did not want to go down the road of converting my thesis into articles for academic journals in order to put my foot on the first rung of the ladder to an academic research career. I therefore looked around for a post which would use my knowledge and skills in a very practical way.'

Subsequent career history

'It took quite a while to manoeuvre myself to where I wanted to be. Having by then a clearer idea of what I wanted to do, I looked very selectively at the job market. Meanwhile I was filling in as a tutorial assistant on a very slender income. I eventually applied successfully for a post as an economic consultant with the Welsh Development Agency, whose clientele is mainly small businesses. My post involves comparative studies of incentives offered by other authorities and investigation of funding from European Union and other sources. My experience of interviewing entrepreneurs and selecting relevant data has proved invaluable when producing Agency reports on the small business sector and user-friendly brochures for business people and potential entrepreneurs.'

Messages from Margaret

'It is important to take your own temperament into account when choosing a career. I knew that I was much happier when I could see that something concrete would happen as a result of my work. I wasn't sure that I would gain the same satisfaction from analysing situations without being able to influence change.

'Who knows? I may yet move further in that direction by becoming a project officer for one of the Agency's urban or rural development programmes. Such a possibility is much more open to me here than it would have been in academia.'

Gerry Gardiner, medical researcher

Background

'I set out on a degree in medicine with the intention of becoming a hospital consultant. In third year, however, I had an opportunity to incorporate an intercalated degree in microbiology and I subsequently decided to specialise in medical research after completing my degree.'

Research experience

'My first research post was in a London medical school in the field of cancer research. I was working with an international team of highly experienced staff and I really felt privileged to be engaged in research which gave me an opportunity to use both of my degrees and to benefit from a stimulating working environment.'

Transition

'After two further contracts and a total of six years in academic research, I still gained personal satisfaction from my work but at the age of twenty-nine I was concerned that I still couldn't get a mortgage because of the insecurity of short-term contracts. I also knew that my salary was less than it would have been had I pursued my original career intention. I was still keen to work in my own field of research but didn't know where to begin to look for another job. In desperation, I decided to visit a graduate careers fair in London to see what options might be open to career changers. My first impression was that the event was geared primarily to recent graduates, but conversations with pharmaceutical companies' representatives subsequently led to a couple of interviews and a job offer in a research and development centre.'

Subsequent career history

'Working in an industrial setting was less of a culture shock than I had imagined. The most attractive aspect was the greater availability of resources if I could justify why I needed them. Certain aspects of the work were different, such as intense scrutiny by the US regulatory authorities before approval of drugs for export. My experience in academic medical research was valuable for joint projects and before long I found myself assisting in the supervision of students on placements from a M.Sc. course in a local university.'

Messages from Gerry

'I would have continued in academic research if I could have made a reasonable living from it. At twenty nine I was concerned that if I didn't make a move soon, I might encounter age limits for entry to other fields. It is all too easy to stick to what is familiar. I had been in universities one way or another for twelve years. It was probably good for me to explore careers in another sector.

'In my experience, research in industry is no less challenging than in universities. The performance appraisal in this company gives me an opportunity to take stock of how I am progressing and how I want to develop my career in future, whereas in the university I didn't look further ahead than gaining an extension of my contract on the same grade'.

Courtney Bonthius, historical researcher

Background

'I took my first degree in liberal arts in the USA and then achieved my dream of coming to Scotland to complete a MA degree in history. My first job was as an historical researcher in an archaeological survey. I loved this work, but the project funding came to an end and I moved on to other work in the voluntary sector and marketing. Along the way I picked up further qualifications in secretarial studies and marketing.'

Research experience

'All along, I really wanted to get back to my first love, history. I was therefore delighted to be offered a fixed term contract as a researcher with a remit to catalogue a Scottish university's historical collection and to contribute to the design and delivery of a postgraduate course in historical studies. The variety made this a potentially challenging and interesting post, but funding for it was very insecure. After a few last minute reprieves, funding finally ceased and my bank balance told me that I really had to re-appraise my situation.'

Transition

'When the university job came to an end, I was stunned and very angry for I had not had prior notice of the ending of my contract. After fuming for a while, I decided that I would only be the loser if I went around with a permanent chip on my shoulder.

'The turning point came quite quickly. One day I simply told myself, 'You are not unemployed. You are self-employed.'

'The next question was, 'self-employed as what?' I asked myself where my strengths lay. I decided that the combination of being an historian and a marketing professional was a saleable asset.'

Subsequent career history

'My husband also has research skills and so we decided to set up an historical research consultancy. The services offered include research for broadcasting and tourism, consultancy and publications for conservation agencies, lectures, production of centenary publications for businesses and computer aided guides to archaeological sites. I am always aware of the need to allow for a sudden down turn in business and we can work on some projects for months before payment is received. To offset this, I continue part-time lecturing in marketing in a local college as a useful source of regular income.'

Messages from Courtney

'I don't regret the change to self-employment. I enjoy being in charge of my own destiny. My advice to anyone contemplating starting a business after a spell in academic research is to be self-motivated and to keep your eye on your goal – a quality which most researchers have developed.

'You will not succeed without a written business plan, and I recommend courses run by local enterprise agencies to help you with the development of your plan and the financial aspects with which you may be unfamiliar.

'Having a business plan does not prevent you from thinking laterally. Indeed, it is essential to be alert to opportunities as they arise. Remember too that you are not the centre of the universe. Not everyone will want your products and services and so there will be setbacks. It is important to keep your sense of humour and perspective. Bring to your business the perseverance which you developed as a researcher and you will not go far wrong.'

Same employer, different occupation

It is not always necessary to change to a different employer in order to develop a career in a new field. The people in this group of case studies diversified their careers while remaining with the same employer.

Morven Campbell, university administrator

Background

'On graduating with a joint honours degree in French and German I had no idea of what I wanted to do next. I knew that I didn't want to teach, but I was aware that my degree in itself did not offer a clear route into a career in business or industry. Knowing that I needed to add some business skills, I took a job with an insurance company in its information services division, which recruited graduates of any discipline to train as programmers. I trained with them for six months and worked for a further year as a programmer. This gave me first-hand experience of IT applications as well as invaluable experience in working for a large multinational company. Programming was not for me. I couldn't get excited about the design of computer code to produce insurance policies, and many of my skills – report writing, social skills and communications – were going unused.'

Research experience

'My next move was to a research centre in a leading business school. I was using my German and my research assistant role involved maintaining information on a European database describing financial incentives. My job was sourcing, translating and maintaining the German information. I found my experience of IT and professional working practice from insurance valuable in this much smaller, research-oriented organisation. The post was interesting and involved fact-finding trips to Germany which both refreshed and enhanced my German.'

Transition

'Although the centre was a distinct entity within the university, I decided to take advantage of opportunities for further study which were open to me as a member of university staff. I knew I was not getting the management training which would have been offered had I remained in insurance and so, to fill this gap, I embarked upon a three year part-time MBA degree, funded by the university.

'I was reasonably happy working in the research centre, but after three years the job became routine. There was little opportunity for progression, When a job came up within the university administration, I decided to apply.'

Subsequent career history

'I became assistant faculty officer for the faculty of engineering, a large and busy faculty within the university. This proved an ideal step. The job required IT experience, good communication skills, the ability and confidence to use initiative and also involved a strong public relations role. The job had a strong service orientation and so it fulfilled my wish for people contact and provided huge variety on a daily basis. I assumed that my MBA degree would be less relevant in this context, but this was not the case. Resource management, presentation skills and strategic management were vital components. The job was continually challenging and offered a great deal of responsibility.

'The transition from small research centre to the administrative hub of the university was as great as if I had changed organisation altogether. In spite of having worked for the university for three years, I was on an extremely steep learning curve regarding the way in which a university is run and the enormous effect of government policies on this. I developed new skills in this job whilst learning a great deal about the business of higher education.'

'After three years in the faculty office, I was promoted to another administrative post, working directly with senior managers, servicing the main decision-making committee of the university. Because I have experience of working in a research unit and a faculty office, I have an ideal background for my job in the central university administration. My own track record gives me a better insight into the needs and priorities of academics.'

Messages from Morven

'There is no such thing as bad experience. However varied a career and seemingly unconnected the steps en route may seem, each piece of experience enhances your ability to respond to the next situation. It's important not to be blinkered and to consider each opportunity on its merits even if it seems unconnected to your current position. I was fortunate in discovering exactly the role I wanted in probably the last place I would have logically looked. Take all training opportunities that present themselves. It all contributes to your professional development and a professional approach is always in demand.'

Catriona Martin, public affairs manager

Background

'I took an honours degree in chemistry, but decided not to follow those of my friends who went straight onto a Ph.D. degree without considering other options. Instead I took on a one year research assistant position. During this year I made full use of courses run by the university for short term contract staff and these were extremely useful when I finally decided to look for a job outside academia.'

Research experience

'Building on the experience gained in research at university, I was recruited by British Nuclear Fuels plc (BNFL). My role was a research associate, working within a team on a research project. I was amazed at the wide range of training opportunities offered by the company to researchers (all at no financial cost to myself). I completed several training courses on communication and team work and gained a practitioner certificate in neuro-linguistic programming. I also spent four months seconded to a plant, gaining experience which I would not get in the research environment. These opportunities opened up my mind to career options which would never have occurred to me had I remained in a university research unit.'

Transition

'After about two years of research work I decided that I was interested in spending time outside research environment. I moved on to another role in BNFL, this time working with a group of people to develop their personal development plans and ensure high quality performance reviews were carried out. This was an extremely interesting and busy role, and allowed me to work with chemists without doing any chemistry myself. I spent one year in this role, and gained a master practitioner qualification in neuro-linguistic programming. I would have been happy to stay in this role for a while longer, but due to budget restrictions I was forced to look for another role.'

Subsequent career history

'I decided that I was not interested in returning to research, and looked at the options available. Drawing on my communications training I found a role in the Public Affairs Group at Sellafield, working within a team looking at ways of improving communication within the company. This has proved an excellent role for gaining a perspective of the company, and allows me to work with a very wide range of people. I also spend roughly one-fifth of my time on a year long fund raising project called Live Challenge '99. This is organised by Border and Granada Television, and I work in a team of five people to raise money which will be used to support local good causes. This provides the opportunity to work with people in the community, and to gain experience of organising large events. It also puts my negotiation skills to the test!'

Messages from Catriona

'I found it helpful to make use of my original qualifications to find a job initially. If you aren't sure you want to continue working in the area of your qualifications, I'd strongly advise looking for a role in a large company. This way, you have the opportunity of moving sideways, or spending time on secondment to gain experience.

'If the opportunity is there to gain additional qualifications, think carefully about what you want to achieve before deciding what you would like to do. The first course you are offered may not be the most appropriate, and you are the best person to know what would benefit you most in the long term.

'As many jobs are never advertised even within a company, if you are interested in moving areas or would like to gain experience through a secondment, the best place to start is by talking to people whom you know. Finding people who have roles which interest you and developing those contacts means that when opportunities come up you'll be well positioned to find out about them.'

Branching out

One of the fascinations of looking at other people's career routes is the realisation of how far afield graduates can branch out from their original degree discipline and still derive satisfaction in their careers. The following case studies are good examples of very wide diversification.

Kenneth Nicholson, business intelligence researcher

Background

'I took my first degree in chemistry before starting employment with the company in which I had enjoyed a summer placement between third and fourth year. Unfortunately, redundancy followed shortly and as a knee-jerk reaction I started an unplanned Ph.D. in chemistry with some reservations. Employment prospects at this time were not great and the offer of a Ph.D. course seemed preferable to unemployment. Following three years of often frustrating research I took a part-time job in the university careers service with the intention of writing my thesis. The part-time employment soon became a full-time (although short-term) administrative job in a pleasant working environment which I really enjoyed.'

Research experience

'Although I had research experience in chemistry, I did not particularly enjoy this type of research and wanted to move away from chemistry. I accepted a seven months contract in another university careers service researching (somewhat ironically) the destinations of graduates from Scottish universities. This was followed by a couple of months' unemployment and miscellaneous administrative work and then another six month contract researching the destinations of contract research staff in Scottish universities. When that contract ended, I bid unsuccessfully for further project funding, but lost out to a well established social science research unit. I then faced another period of unemployment.'

Transition

'The transition came for me when I realised that I could not depend on getting contracts for the rest of my life without intermittent periods of unemployment. I had reached a stage in my life where I needed a steady income. The thrill of getting a new contract is great at the time, but a couple of months on the dole soon knocks the wind out of your sails.

'I decided to try employment outside the university environment and even when I heard someone was asking after me about another research contract, I decided not to contact him.'

Subsequent career history

'I now work with a management consultancy, researching opportunities for developing new business areas, a job I secured through a contact at the university. I have found that the skills acquired from research experience are tremendously useful in this job and I enjoy the relative security it provides.'

Messages from Kenneth

'Try to make the most of every job you do, however trivial it may seem. I started a part-time job in a university careers service stuffing envelopes. I believe my positive attitude and enthusiasm for a job which many may have thought beneath them brought rewards of further work and a subsequent research contract. This was assisted by making numerous contacts and creating a network of people looking out for possible opportunities for me.

'Every single job I have had since graduating has been through contacts. I have not followed a formal career path as I decided not to pursue my degree subject. In a sense, having a degree can blinker you. You feel you should look only for opportunities in that field, but don't be afraid to try something different.'

Moira McMillan, IT trainer and information manager

Background

'I came to academic research relatively late in life, following an M.Sc. in information management. Before then, I had been a civil servant for eleven years and self-employed for four years after taking my first degree in economics.'

Research experience

'The world didn't seem to be waiting eagerly for me to graduate and so I was glad to accept a short-term contract to write a guide to job search on the Internet for contract research staff at a university careers service. This involved reviewing Web-sites and interviewing focus groups of researchers. Upon completion of the guide, I trained information managers and staff from careers services around the UK in the use of the Internet to assist job seekers.'

Transition

'When my contract ended, I realised that I had two potentially valuable areas of experience for self-employment: using the Internet and training. I decided to apply to my local enterprise trust for use of an 'incubation unit' for three months to explore setting up an Internet training company. Unfortunately, family problems intervened and I had to give up the unit. However, my solicitor encouraged me to continue with the idea of offering Internet training and suggested that professional firms could be a good starting point. I decided to try out the idea, this time working from home to minimise costs.'

Subsequent career history

'I realised that I wanted a professional qualification in training and enrolled on the Institute of Personnel and Development's Certificate in Training Practice. I also undertook self-training to bring my computer skills up to required levels. I began to offer word processing and keyboard skills courses, as well as Internet training. Problems arose when people showed interest in the courses, but were unable to find time to fit them into their busy schedules. There could be a delay of weeks or even months between initial contact and actually carrying out the training. I enjoyed what I was doing, but realised that I had to diversify in order to boost my income.

'I began with abstracting work which I could carry out by teleworking and made applications for jobs, both part-time and full-time. Fortunately, a part-time post in an information technology project in a university library gave me security of income for three years, while leaving me free to pursue Internet training as a secondary activity.

'It also leaves me free to pick up "one off" contracts, such as website design for an enterprise agency and I am happy with a portfolio career, with elements of contract work and self-employment. I have realised that I don't want to incur the financial risks of setting up a company.'

Messages from Moira

'If you are interested in self-employment, it is useful to remember that there are many ways of being self-employed. You do not have to be an "entrepreneur" and risk your house and assets in borrowing money. You can combine elements of self-employment with contract work or part-time work.

'Training and keeping qualifications up to date are very important, both to enhance your portfolio of skills and give you confidence that whatever you are offering is based on current knowledge and best practice. I would also recommend that you join any professional associations and mailing lists relevant to your field. They can be useful sources of opportunities and new ideas.'

Simon Chalmers, holiday manager

Background

'I took a BA in medical sciences and went on to complete three years of clinical studies in veterinary medicine, gaining a MA but failing the Final Surgery Examination and so not achieving professional status as MRCVS. A rare type of glaucoma in my left eye had been progressing and the eye became totally blind and was removed. This long struggle with no end result led to depression and a loss of direction. Seeking to bring at least some of the scientific training into use, I went on to complete a post graduate diploma course in biotechnology.'

Research experience

'This led to a research position at Enzymatix on the Cambridge Science Park in veterinary-related aspects of the field, which I enjoyed. Biotechnology development involves investments of high-risk capital, however, and the company, although successful, had to give up its lab space for the "next big thing", in this case, optical isomer production studies.'

Transition

'After this disappointment, it seemed time to retreat from a world of relatively high achievements which had all come to nothing. I spent a year living peacefully on a houseboat in Cornwall with my wife and family. After enjoying the idyll, a drive emerged to achieve something, take part, give back.'

Subsequent career hxistory

'Two hundred job applications targeted at relevant posts throughout the southwest brought little response. I didn't want to move out of the area and so I had to take a fresh look at my situation.

'92 per cent of the economy of Cornwall is based on tourism and tourism needs well trained people. I got a job doing market research for a time share company, which led to a team leader post in tele-canvassing and subsequently to a managerial post on a holiday resort with thirty-five holiday homes, a hotel, a leisure centre and a golf course.'

Messages from Simon

'Avoid the "holy grail syndrome". If one career path is not working out, it is best to adapt and move on. Although demanding and stressful at times, my job suits me. I spent too long chasing an ideal and should have reassessed matters more frequently and more deeply. If you find you're good at something and happy doing it, just keep working at it and you'll find success comes easily. It doesn't have to be the job of your dreams.

'Medical problems need not stop you from succeeding. Mental health problems associated with my failure to become a vet have receded over the years as I have enjoyed my life in tourism. A disfigured eye led to shyness of eye contact (vital for job interviews), but surgery and a good prosthesis put this right.'

Allan Grant, health trust chief executive

Background

'I gained a first degree in economic history before taking research leading to a Ph.D. degree. At this time I was not clear about a career direction, but was motivated by interest in my topic of research.'

Research experience

'I obtained a three year grant for research into the impact of war on the Scottish economy, 1750–1830. During this time I did some teaching and tutoring work. Nearing the end of the period covered by my grant, I had to consider my next move.'

Transition

'Seeing limited academic career opportunities and wishing to combine my interest in public sector economics with a professional career, I thought that the National Audit Office (NAO) seemed to offer a sensible combination. I felt that a professional qualification would stand me in good stead and keep future career options open. I therefore joined the NAO, undertaking professional studies to become a chartered public finance accountant.

'As in the case of many Ph.Ds, I had reams of research material at the end of my research grant, but most of the writing up was outstanding. Undertaking professional studies and starting a new career meant that little was done on the Ph.D. for nine months. I then spent a busy year completing and submitting the Ph.D. whilst undertaking accounting exams at the same time – a challenging year, with little social life!'

Subsequent career history

'I stayed with the NAO for five years until I reached another crossroads, to make a career as an auditor or branch into another area. The health service seemed to offer fresh challenges for accountants interested in general management. From the NAO I joined the National Health Service, filling a series of finance and general management posts. I am now chief executive of a NHS trust, having been previously a director of finance, a useful background for my current role.'

Messages from Allan

'I had never really set my sights on an academic career, but I took a bit of a gamble undertaking accountancy exams with a Ph.D. to finish. Fortunately, I was able to do both partly because I was determined, an essential attribute for a researcher! It is important to be clear about which skills you want to transfer from one context to another; relevance is the key. Research provides you with a number of tools which you can apply in any situation, particularly in relation to problem solving. At the same time promoting a learning culture is critical to the success of large complex organisations and again research skills are transferable.'

Thinking points

Interesting though it is to read about the career progress of other researchers, it is valuable only if you can apply their messages to your own circumstances. This chapter therefore ends with a number of questions drawn from the case studies. Your answers to these questions will help you to clarify your own thinking and so to progress your career planning. In answering these questions you can draw upon your responses in exercises earlier in this book.

Pause to take stock

In one way or another all of the people in the case studies stopped in their tracks to take stock of their circumstances and to confront honestly their feelings about where they were going (or not going in some cases). By reading this book you have come to a similar crossroads in your career.

- What options do you see, branching out from this point in your career?
- If you are honest with yourself, which one is most attractive?
- Is the most attractive option feasible, given your circumstances?
- If it is feasible, what – if anything – is preventing you from taking up that option?
- If it is not feasible, what would be an acceptable compromise solution?

Take account of your temperament

Several of the graduates performed well in various occupations, but felt that these were not best suited to their temperament or that certain aspects of their personality – often inter-personal skills – were not fully used in what they were doing. They had a sense that they could find a more natural environment for their temperament elsewhere.

- What adjectives would you use to describe your temperament?
- Is it well matched to what you are doing now?
- What aspects of your temperament – if any – are not well matched in your current occupation?
- What type of work would more fully accommodate your temperament?

Have confidence in your transferable skills

All of the people in the case studies identified ways in which their research skills helped them in a very diverse range of occupations. They cited skills such as planning, organisation of materials and tasks, time management, critical analysis, problem solving, communication and negotiation. They also drew confidence from the fact that they had successfully completed intellectually challenging research and could transfer the techniques required in doing that to completely different spheres.

- How do you rate your ability in the range of skills identified by the researchers?
- What other skills would you add to this list, based on your experience?
- What evidence of these skills can you produce to back your claims?
- What is the most challenging research which you have successfully completed?
- How will the learning gained through that research stand you in good stead for the future?

Be determined and resilient

Most of the graduates suffered setbacks and disappointments. Several of them also had to undertake excessive workloads in order to gain additional professional qualifications while working full-time. On the whole, good researchers are determined, resilient people who do not give up easily. Perhaps you have not thought of this characteristic as being an asset when applied to career planning.

- When have you suffered setbacks and disappointments, in both work and life in general?
- What internal and external factors enable you to overcome these?
- If you were to change direction now, what would be the worst thing which could happen?
- If that worst-case scenario occurred, how would you deal with it?
- Where could you turn for support if that were to happen?
- How likely is the worst-case scenario to happen?
- Does this line of thinking convince you that it would be wise not to proceed in this direction, or does it make the calculated risk seem more acceptable?

Reap the rewards of boldness

Even those of the graduates who suffered setbacks can look back now and say that they arrived at a more satisfactory point in their career through making a change. For some this has brought promotion and financial gain. For others the primary gains have been independence and a better quality of life. Individuals seek different rewards from work and so career planning should be directed towards achieving what matters to you.

- What rewards do you gain from your work now, and would like to continue in future employment?
- What rewards which are important to you are not satisfied in your present job?
- What kind of work would be most likely to give you those kinds of rewards?
- Would that work also incorporate the rewards gained from your present work?
- On balance, would the risks and effort required to reap the rewards be justified?

None of these case studies may be an exact role model for you, but it is encouraging to remember that these are all real people and it is helpful to see that success can come in many ways. The path leading to success may not always be smooth, but difficulties can be overcome through perseverance. With this encouragement you can now turn to focus on getting a job.

Part IV

Focus on getting a job

Chapter 9

Finding vacancies

Most people equate finding vacancies with seeing jobs advertised in newspapers. If, however, you conduct a survey of how you and your friends have found jobs in the past, you will probably come up with quite a range of methods. What may surprise you is how many vacancies were not publicly advertised. Indeed, recruitment consultants have estimated that up to 60 per cent of vacancies are not advertised, and this proportion increases for older applicants.

It is important, then, that you should know about both advertised and unadvertised vacancies. This chapter will advise you how to find out about both, for academic and other jobs.

Advertised vacancies

Academic vacancies

There are some regular publications in which academic posts are traditionally advertised:

- The *Times Higher Education Supplement* (Fridays)
- *The Guardian* (education supplement)
- Major regional papers in the location of the university, in Scotland, for example, *The Herald* and *The Scotsman*.

If it is hoped to attract an international pool of applicants or if the post is overseas, it may also be advertised via the Association of Commonwealth Universities which distributes vacancies to UK universities. These may be displayed in either the personnel office, the careers service or the university library.

Depending on the nature of the research or teaching vacancy, it may also be advertised in a specialist journal or a professional magazine. For instance:

- many scientific posts are advertised in the *New Scientist*
- a lecturing post in human resource management might be advertised in *People Management*, the journal of the Institute of Personnel and Development.

Temporary posts on the lower range of the research assistant scale may be advertised internally. You may enquire about such posts either directly to a department or at the personnel office. They may also be advertised in university staff magazines.

It is also worth keeping an eye on announcements in papers such as *The Times Higher Education Supplement* and in staff magazines of research awards granted to departments. It is possible that all the staff for the funded project are already in place, but sometimes an award of funding may herald a new appointment.

Other advertised vacancies

Practitioners should be able to tell you where vacancies are normally advertised. With their help, draw up your own checklist using the following framework.

- National newspapers: find out on which day of the week the types of post in which you are interested are regularly advertised.
- Professional journals: if you do not know in which journals to look for a specific type of vacancy, use *Willing's Press Guide* in a library to guide you to appropriate publications.
- Vacancy bulletins: although intended for finalists and recent graduates, vacancy bulletins produced by the Higher Education Careers Services Unit (CSU) and university careers services may alert you to either vacancies which would suit you or employers' interests which you might want to pursue via a speculative letter.

Vacancies on the Internet

There is increasing use of the Internet for advertising vacancies in many kinds of organisations. Sometimes these repeat vacancies which are also advertised in the press. For example, vacancies advertised in *The Times Higher Education Supplement* on a Friday are accessible on the Internet from the previous Tuesday. In other instances, the Internet may be the sole means of advertising a vacancy, on the assumption that the right kind of candidate would be regularly browsing in the Internet. This is particularly the case for computing and other technological vacancies.

It is possible to waste an enormous amount of time surfing aimlessly around the Internet and so it is useful to have a few guidelines. *The Guide to Job Seeking via the Internet for Academic Researchers*, produced by the Scottish Graduate Careers Partnership (1997 and updated in 1998), was designed specifically with contract research staff in mind and it is a good starting point. It should be available in most university careers services, and is also available on the Internet at http://www.strath.ac.uk/Departments/Careers/guide/

Vacancies overseas

Seeking vacancies overseas is much easier than once was the case, thanks to the Internet. Not all jobs will be advertised in this way, however, and it is useful to know of some starting points in addition to obvious sources such as national newspapers and professional journals.

- Contact the High Commission or Embassy of the country where you would like to work for information on the likelihood of a foreign national being recruited. This will depend on skill shortages and work permit regulations.
- If the answer is promising, the Embassy may be able to tell you how such vacancies would be advertised.
- The British Council is a good source of information on posts with an academic or cultural slant. This is particularly suitable if you want a short term post overseas.
- The Department of International Development deals with a wider range of skilled occupations and consultancy posts in response to requests from developing countries.
- Contact the UK branch of multi-national companies to find out whether they recruit for overseas divisions of their organisation. If they do not, they should be able to give you a contact overseas whom you can contact direct.
- The university from which you graduated and the one in which you currently work may have alumni branches overseas, or at least may know of individual alumni in the country where you would like to work. Such contacts could be a starting point for an enquiry about the local labour market.
- Some recruitment agencies specialise in finding positions overseas for registrants. They may focus either on particular countries or particular types of work. Look at the *Executive Grapevine* directory for advice on which agencies are likely to meet your needs.
- It would be impossible to list all the books which deal with finding employment overseas, but the following sources of information (not all designed primarily for job seekers) may be helpful:

> *How to Get a Job Abroad*
> *Live and Work in America* (also *Australia, Belgium, France, Germany, Italy, Saudi Arabia, Spain,* etc.)
> *Finding Work Overseas*
> *The Directory of Work and Study in Developing Countries*
> *The Directory of Jobs and Careers Abroad*
> *Obtaining Visas and Work Permits.*

Further details of these publications are given in the bibliography. In addition to these suggestions, the methods of finding unadvertised vacancies outlined in the following section apply in principle also to overseas posts.

The hidden job market

Before looking at sources of unadvertised vacancies, it is necessary to air a few concerns which some job seekers have about this type of vacancy. They may feel that there is something slightly underhand about vacancies not being advertised, and that the practice flies in the face of equal opportunities. Very occasionally that may indeed be the case, but in most cases it is a method adopted in order to keep the number of candidates to a manageable proportion and to secure an appointment more rapidly than it could have been achieved through the long process of advertising and waiting for applications to come in by a closing date. It can also be a way of securing candidates on the recommendation of a trusted intermediary, thus giving the employer an assurance that the appointment will be successful.

How, then, do you find out about sources of unadvertised vacancies? The following section outlines some of the main ways of accessing the hidden job market.

Internal vacancies

Once you are working inside an organisation, even on a temporary basis you may be in a position to see internal vacancy advertisements. If you are interested in remaining in the organisation, find out at an early stage how vacancies are advertised. It may be on a noticeboard at the personnel office or some other central location, or via a staff newsletter or bulletin. Such posts are usually open to temporary staff.

If you are not yet working in an organisation, but you have a contact who works there, it is worth asking to see any internal vacancies which might suit you. There is no guarantee that an application from an external applicant will be considered for an internal vacancy, but if you seem ideally suited for a particular vacancy, it is certainly worth making the effort or at least ringing the personnel officer to state your case in a convincing manner.

Agencies

Depending on the relevance of your experience and the type of vacancy which you are seeking, it may be useful to be registered with appropriate recruitment agencies. You should be realistic about what to expect from agencies. Remembering that since employers pay agencies a fee to find them suitable candidates, it is understandable that agencies:

- rarely have vacancies for people with no relevant experience or qualifications
- tend to adhere very strictly to the essential and desirable criteria laid down by employers
- are not often used by certain types of organisations, including universities, health service trusts and local government.

In the past it was true that agencies also did not handle the types of posts for which employers could expect to receive huge numbers of applications, for example, an entry level post in personnel management with a 'blue-chip' company. Recently, however, some major recruiters have outsourced the initial phase of selection to agencies because they have reduced their own staffing in their personnel department.

If you decide to use agencies, it is important to find those which are appropriate to your discipline and the type of work which you are seeking. You could languish for a long time on an agency's books if, for instance, you are seeking a technical vacancy and their speciality is in marketing. A reputable agency will not accept you if the staff think that they are unlikely to have vacancies to match your profile and so it is rarely worth insisting on being registered.

To identify the agencies relevant to your job search you can use the following sources:

- *Yellow Pages* for the area where you wish to be located
- *Executive Grapevine*
- *Directory of Recruitment Consultancies.*

A few other hints will help you to make the most of this source of vacancies.

- Do not pay to register with an agency. Reputable agencies gain their income from fees earned from employers and do not charge potential employees.
- Do not register with an agency and sit back, thinking that this will take care of your job search. Use it as one method alongside others in your job search strategy.
- Keep in contact regularly with the agency (or agencies) with which you are registered. Naturally, the staff will bring you to mind more readily for vacancies if you are in touch regularly on a polite, friendly basis than they can if you are simply a name on a file.
- Be clear about the types of vacancies and the locations that you will or will not consider so that your name is not put forward for inappropriate vacancies.
- At the same time do not be too prescriptive about what you will consider or else you may remain in the agency's filing cabinet for a very long time.

Speculative applications

People tend to divide into two camps on speculative applications. Those who have sent off hundreds of letters to no avail dismiss the process as a complete waste of time and wonder why careers advisers suggest it. On the other hand, people who have had an amazing 'lucky break' after one or two approaches to employers think that this is a superb method of job hunting and wonder why every job seeker does not adopt it.

The truth lies somewhere in the middle. If up to 60 per cent of vacancies are unadvertised, it does not make sense to rely solely on newspaper advertisements, especially when there are numerous applicants for every advertised vacancy. The secret is not to send off speculative letters on a purely random basis, but to target organisations which you have reason to believe might have vacancies. But how can you know which organisations to target?

Contacts

A good source of inside information are the contacts whom you listed in chapter 6 when you were seeking basic careers information. Consult them again about where and when vacancies might arise. Sometimes they may tell you that the market is absolutely flat, or that the industry is going through a 'down-sizing' phase with consequent redundancies. On the other hand, they may know whose business is doing well and who has recently won good contracts, which may require more staff, even on a temporary basis.

Economic reviews

Check out economic reviews on particular industries or geographic areas. These will tell you which sectors are buoyant and which are limping along. Such reviews may be found in the following sources, and no doubt your contacts can tell you of others for the area of interest to you:

- *Labour Market Quarterly*, published by the Department for Education and Employment
- regional reviews by TECs and LECS
- journals of chambers of commerce
- reports of economic monitoring units in universities, such as the Fraser of Allander Institute (University of Strathclyde), the Institute of Employment Research (University of Warwick)
- *The Financial Times*
- *The Economist*
- *Income Data Services Survey*
- the business pages of the quality press, which often quote from some of the more extensive sources listed above.

Press cuttings file

It is a good idea to keep a press cuttings file to remind you of likely sources of vacancies when you come to write speculative applications. You can collect articles from professional journals, but even the daily newspapers can be sources of useful information which may suggest that a speculative application could be profitable. The type of information which you are looking out for could be along the following lines:

- reasons given for movements in stocks and shares. Is an upsurge due to recent expansion plans?
- reviews of companies' annual reports, stating their viability and future plans
- announcements of promotions, which may suggest vacancies lower down the ladder
- reports of awards for exporting or other activities, which suggest that organisations are leaders in their field
- news articles about orders for work secured by companies.

A signal of this kind could be a cue for a well worded speculative application, drawing on the facts which you have gathered to form a knowledgeable opinion to your introductory letter (see chapter 11).

At the same time, your scrutiny of the press may alert you to organisations which are struggling and to which it would be a waste of time to send a speculative letter. A few examples of alarm bells are given below:

- notification of redundancies because of lack of orders or cuts in public service expenditure.
- consequences of mergers. Buy-outs and mergers can sometimes create more jobs, but very frequently there may be a weeding out of staff and a recruitment freeze until the merger process has been assimilated
- natural or political phenomena which affect particular industries or countries, such as a world crop failure, a disruption in fuel supplies or civil unrest which sends the value of a nation's currency plummeting.

These are a few suggestions on ways of ensuring that your speculative applications are well targeted. You may be able to think of other sources of reliable information within your own field. It is all based on thinking around the subject of your job search, a process in which researchers are well schooled. Apply this skill to your job search and you are likely to be successful.

Success, however, also depends on having very professional looking credentials to place before employers. We therefore turn in chapter 10 to the important topic of CVs and covering letters.

Chapter 10

Presenting your case
CVs and covering letters

A curriculum vitae has been described as 'the most important document you will ever write'. In many respects that is true as your CV can be the key to a job which will shape a large part of your life.

Given the importance of the CV, however, it is amazing how much ignorance there is about its purpose and content among otherwise intelligent people. Before looking in detail at the content of a CV, let's spend some time thinking about its purpose and some basic 'do's' and 'don'ts'.

Purpose of a CV

A CV is a presentation to an employer of selected facts about yourself which are relevant to a particular post or a type of post.

Points to note

- 'A presentation' suggests that the CV is well laid out and is in a logical order with bold headings to guide the reader's eye through the text. Appearance at first sight matters a great deal in a CV.
- 'Selected facts' means that you are not obliged to cite every activity from babyhood to the present day.
- 'Relevant to a particular post' suggests that a good CV should be targeted for specific purposes. A multi-purpose CV suitable for any occasion is a myth which is not worth pursuing. If you intend to apply for more than one type of post, you will need to re-focus your CV, perhaps only slightly, but significantly.

Do's and don'ts

To achieve the best results do:

- try to keep your CV to two A4 pages, typed on one side
- add publications, conference papers, a research synopsis on an extra page (if appropriate)

- use quality paper in white or a pale, neutral colour
- use a laser printer with black ink or a dark colour which will photocopy well
- provide a cover or folder which will keep your CV pristine when others look crumpled
- leave some white space in the layout to relieve the reader's eye
- use bullet point format in places to avoid huge blocks of text
- check and double-check spelling, punctuation and grammar and ask a reliable friend to make a final check.

To avoid common pitfalls, do not:

- cram every centimetre of your two pages with detailed facts
- begin your CV with the words 'Curriculum Vitae' in huge bold letters, followed by your name in microscopic print
- write your CV in the third person
- allocate space inappropriately to unimportant facts (e.g. details of school qualifications when you are on a post-doctoral fellowship)
- make unsubstantiated claims about your merits without providing solid evidence
- give long lists of duties without reference to skills acquired through doing them.

Preparing to write a CV

Before compiling your CV, there is work to be done on scrap paper. Ideally, you should assemble the following items before you begin:

- Details of your qualifications with dates of award
- Details of the vacancy for which you are applying (if appropriate)
- The information which you have gathered on the type of post for which you are applying.

Stage 1: Identifying the employer's criteria

If you are applying for a particular post, highlight all the key words in the job description which indicate what the employer is looking for. If you are applying speculatively or do not have a job description, write down all the criteria which from your investigation of this type of post you think that the employer will consider to be essential and desirable. Once you have identified what you consider to be the employer's main criteria , write them down the left hand side of a page.

Stage 2: Gathering your evidence

The most important thing about a CV is that it should not be a series of vague claims, but should be grounded in solid evidence which proves that you are not only a suitable, but an excellent candidate. Time spent on accumulating your evidence before writing your CV will pay dividends.

Returning to the diagram in which you have entered the employer's criteria, write down all the personal evidence which you can muster. You may not use it all in a particular CV, but for the moment write it all down. You will no doubt find that in some areas you have an abundance of evidence and for the CV you will be able to select the best and most relevant examples. In other areas, however, you may be deficient and this is where you may have to tax your brains, and possibly call on friends who may recall something which you have forgotten. It is not always possible to have evidence for every single criterion, but if there are too many blank spaces or examples of weak evidence, you may want to reconsider whether there is any point in applying. The examples which follow may help you to understand the kinds of evidence which you can use.

Example

Jill has completed a Ph.D. in environmental planning and has been working as a research assistant on an environmental project in a department of urban and regional planning. Her other work experience includes summer jobs in a tourist board and a play leader in a children's summer camp. Her interests include voluntary conservation work in the countryside, various sports, theatre, cinema and concerts.

Jill wishes to apply for a post as a development officer with a local enterprise agency. The post involved applications for funding to the European Union and other funding bodies, designing projects which improve the environment in the broadest possible sense, and overseeing projects from start up to completion. The evidence which Jill can draw up is described in Table 10.1.

Some of the elements of Jill's evidence are more substantial than others, but by drawing on her academic studies, her work experience and her interests she has managed to give some reasonable kinds of evidence opposite every criterion which she thinks may be important to the employer.

Points to note

Select what is relevant

She can now go back over the evidence before transferring it to her CV and decide which parts are most relevant and will present her in the best light. For instance, under supervisory skills it may be that her work with conservation volunteers is most similar to the work which she would do as a development officer. She may therefore decide not the use the example relating to supervision of undergraduates if she has very little experience of that. She is mindful that in the CV she will have only two pages to display her best selling points and she must therefore be selective.

Table 10.1 Matching evidence to job requirements

Job requirements	My evidence
Analytical ability	Analysis of masses of data and ability to extract what is relevant – from Ph.D. study
Creativity	Ph.D. is original work Inventing amusements for children at summer camp
Written communication	Long reports – Ph.D. thesis Short, formal reports – articles in planning journals Publicity leaflets – for Student Conservation Group

Oral communication	Formal – speaker at planning conferences
	    – presenting papers in tutorial groups
	Informal– dealing with public in tourist board
	    – variety of communication at summer camp (giving instructions, drama, story-telling)

Forward planning	Working out own schedule for Ph.D.. Working out resource requirements and timetable for current project
Organisational skills	Organising focus groups to gather public opinion on current project Organising an entire summer programme of activities for children
Ability to monitor progress	Review meetings built into both Ph.D. studies and current project
Team work	Co-operative member of a small project team in Planning Department Member of a team for rowing and relay running Work with other volunteers in conservation projects Co-operated with other play-leaders at summer camp Tourist Board team gave mutual back-up
Ability to handle finance	Accountable for part of the budget for current project – £15,000 (12% of total budget)
Fund raising	Involved in charity fund-raising for conservation groups – campaign raised £25,000 Aware of project team leader's bids to funding bodies
Persuasive ability	Recruitment of new members for Student Conservation Group Sustaining thesis before examiners at viva for Ph.D. Presenting reports on current project to project sponsors
Supervisory skills	Occasional tutorial work with undergraduates Supervising younger volunteers on conservation projects Responsible for safety, welfare and discipline of 20 children at summer camp

Make the most of your evidence

Note how Jill has made the most of those parts of her evidence where her experience could be slender by comparison with that of other candidates. She does not have experience of securing large grants from funding authorities, which could be a weak point. To counteract this problem, Jill has been careful to quantify the total amount of money raised in the fundraising campaign in which she was involved and the portion of the project budget for which she is accountable. These give an indication that she has been associated with securing and managing reasonably large sums of money. Mention of awareness of the bidding process within the department demonstrates that she knows what is involved even though she has not been personally responsible for it.

Be specific

Jill avoids bland generalisations in favour of more specific evidence. For instance, she could have used headings such as 'Finance' and 'Communication Skills', but she broke these topics into sub-headings which enabled her to give much more detailed evidence of the full range of her abilities and experience in these areas.

Bearing in mind the way in which Jill tackled the process of gathering evidence, do the same for yourself in relation to a particular advertised post or a type of post for which you intend to apply on a speculative basis. Write the employer's criteria and your evidence in Exercise 10.1.

Stage 3: Summarise your evidence

By now you may be aware that you have more evidence than you will ever get on to a two-page CV. That is no bad thing as the process of gathering your evidence helps to build up your confidence. It is good to know that you have evidence in reserve and you can afford to select the best and most relevant demonstrations of your competence and suitability when applying for a post.

Before moving onto the construction of a CV, go back over your evidence diagram and highlight those items which are most appropriate for inclusion in your CV. These are the fundamental building blocks which you must incorporate into the CV in order to do yourself justice.

We shall return to Jill and your own evidence shortly, but first we need to look at the basic structure of a CV.

Content of a curriculum vitae

There is no single correct format for a CV, as will become apparent as this chapter proceeds. There are, however, certain conventions in CV writing, and also some bad practices which are best avoided. This section gives a brief outline of the normal content of a CV, followed by some examples of good and bad practice.

Exercise 10.1 Gathering evidence

Job requirements	My evidence

Main sections of a CV

Personal details

This section need not be headed with the words 'curriculum vitae'. Sometimes these words dominate the front page of a CV to no benefit whatsoever.

Keep this section simple. It can look very effective to have your name centred and in bold type, with your address and means of communication (telephone number, e-mail, fax) tucked underneath your name. If you have two addresses, put them to opposite sides at the top of the page and indicate clearly when you can be reached at each address.

These are the only essentials in this section. Everything else is optional.

- Date of birth is commonly added. This is a reasonable addition, but you do not need your age as well. Older candidates should be aware that adding a date of birth may not do them any favours in view of age discrimination, which is rampant in some areas. If as an older candidate you want to give your date of birth, you may prefer to tuck it away at the end of the CV rather than displaying it in the very first section.

- Nationality may be important if either you are applying for a post where you have to be of a specific nationality or the employer needs to know that you are not a native of the country in which you are applying for a job. If you know that you definitely do not need a work permit, it is worth stating that in case employers otherwise would not give your application serious consideration. If, however, you are a native of the country in which you are applying and it is obvious from your CV that you have always lived in that country, it is probably unnecessary to state your nationality.
- Gender need not be stated if your name indisputably applies exclusively to either men or women. If, however, your name could apply to either gender or is a name from overseas which may not be recognised by employers, you can state either your title (if it is gender specific) or your gender.
- State of health is another fact which often appears among personal details, but again it is not strictly necessary. The assumption is that you are in good health. If there are any health or disability issues, it may be better to make a separate statement about these in a very positive manner rather than including them in your CV, which is a presentation of you in your professional persona.
- Marital status is another unnecessary piece of information. Very rarely is marital status a condition of gaining employment and it is therefore not necessary to comment on it unless this has been specifically requested by an employer, which is unusual.
- Other details such as national insurance number and the ages of children often appear at this point in CVs. These are an unnecessary distraction from the other important information which should be prominent on page one.

Career goal

This is an optional section. If you are applying for a university research post very similar to one which you have at present, or moving between any two posts which are closely related, you may consider that a career goal statement is superfluous. On the other hand, if you are trying to make a transition into a different kind of career, a career goal statement can focus your CV and help to persuade the employer that you have given serious thought to your next move.

A career goal statement consists of:

- an indication of where you are trying to reach in your career
- succinct details of the skills which will take you there.

Example

Career goal: To develop a career as a technical author for engineering products, based on my strong academic background in engineering and my demonstrated ability to communicate appropriately in writing with various client groups.

The hints given in the career goal statement would then have to be substantiated in the body of the CV. By seeing them flagged up at the start, the reader feels that this CV may be worth reading and knows what evidence to look out for in other sections of the CV.

Education

Education may come next on your CV, but if you feel that your work experience is more relevant, you can reverse the order of these two sections. Relevance is always the driving force in CV construction.

Reverse chronology is the normal way to present your education, but there are other methods. For instance, you may choose to divide this section into academic and professional qualifications, with the emphasis on whichever category seems more important for a particular post.

Be sensible about your allocation of space. If you are a postdoctoral fellow, most employers will not be the least bit interested in your 'O' level, Standard Grade or GCSE passes. A few employers (e.g. accountants) still ask about UCAS points from school leaving qualifications, but unless this is specifically mentioned, you can safely assume that if you have a higher degree, you may omit school qualifications unless you particularly want to include mention of a language or evidence of numeracy if these competences are not obvious from your later studies.

The amount of details which you should include on your higher education depends very much on the type of post which you are seeking and what you are trying to prove.

- For an academic post you will want to give a fair amount of detail of the breadth and depth of your studies in your discipline. You may wish to supplement this with a synopsis of your research as an appendix to your CV.
- For a non-academic post the balance of what you include in the education section of your CV will be determined by whether you think the employer will be more interested in your subject knowledge, or the transferable skills gained from your academic studies.

For instance, if you have completed a Ph.D. in Scottish shipbuilding in the nineteenth century and are now applying for a post as a civil service research officer, rather than giving minute details of your research topic, it would be more useful to cite some of the skills acquired. For example:

- ability to assimilate vast quantities of data and extract relevant facts
- capacity for understanding, generating and interpreting complex statistics
- ability to construct a database on computer

- good written communication skills, with an emphasis on precision and clarity of language
- ability to construct and defend a logical presentation of your findings.

Work experience

This section can have various names, such as 'Employment' or 'Career History'. You can choose a heading to suit yourself, but 'Work Experience' is sufficiently broad to encompass work for which you were not paid, but which you may wish to mention.

You also have choices as to how you construct this section. The commonest formats are given below.

Reverse chronology

There is little to be gained from having your job as a sixteen-year-old waitress emblazoned across page one while your experience as a research assistant only emerges half way down page two. As with education the order in which you present your various jobs and the amount of space which you allocate to each should reflect what is relevant to an employer. On that basis you may decide to omit the school holidays waitressing job. On the other hand, if you need to demonstrate the ability to give good customer service, that job could be a cumulative piece of evidence in your favour.

Employment themes

Sometimes it is preferable to group your jobs in themes rather than in strict reverse chronological order. This can be handy in the following situations:

- If you have been doing a 'stop-gap' job in an unrelated field since the end of your last research contract, you may want to have a 'Research' heading appearing first in your employment section.
- If you have had a variety of jobs for short periods, interspersed with non-relevant occupations, you may prefer to create some groupings to show that, for instance, you have had five years' experience of information management related work, even though it has not been gained in a continuous block.
- The thematic method can be used as a space saver where listing every single job of a particular kind would use up a whole page. For example:

   'Additional experience has included part-time catering work over six years. This has enhanced my ability to give friendly, efficient service to customers, even when working under pressure in busy restaurants with discriminating clientele.'

Whichever of these formats you prefer, you need to decide what points you wish to bring out from this important section of your CV. Skills and achievements are two of the important messages which you want to get across to employers. You can build these into your CV in various ways:

- within your description of each job you can make a statement about the associated skills and achievements, probably in the form of bullet points in order to avoid having dense blocks of text
- alternatively, you can state your various jobs briefly and follow on with separate sections on skills and achievements, drawing on those gained from several jobs.

Either way can be effective if you observe the following 'do's' and 'don'ts':

Do:
- Choose to highlight skills which are relevant to the occupation sought. There is little point in elaborating on the writing of lengthy reports if the core of the job you want is about negotiation skills.
- Wherever possible quantify and specify information which will give a clearer picture of the context in which you have worked. For example, if you 'conducted a project for major clients':
  - what do you mean by 'conducted'? What specifically was your role?
  - was it a two week or a two year long project?
  - was it a £5,000 or a £5,000,000 project?
  - in what sector were these clients? Can you mention some by name?

Do not:
- give turgid repetition of lists of duties which were similar in several jobs, particularly where these are irrelevant to the post for which you are applying
- lapse into rhetoric in the third person about a particular occupation or industry in which you have worked. For example, 'Project management is a challenging and demanding occupation in which managers have to be . . .' The emphasis should be on you and what you have done. Own your acquired skills and don't lose sight of them in third person narrative.

Positions of responsibility

This is an optional section. You may feel that your positions of responsibility are adequately covered in other sections of your CV. However, if the post for which you are applying calls for you to exercise responsibility in a greater degree than you have experienced hitherto, you may prefer the cumulative effect of drawing your experience from several aspects of your life together into a single section which demonstrates your potential. Examples can be drawn from leisure, work and study activities. They may relate to one off activities (e.g. organisation of a single event such as a meeting of postgraduate students with Teaching Quality Assessors) as well as continuing offices of responsibility in a society.

Achievements

This is also optional. If you have spelled out your achievements section by section, it could be overkill to repeat them here, but if it is important to give an image of being a high achiever for a particularly competitive post, this can be a way of accumulating disparate pieces of information which build up such an image.

Examples of the type of information which you can include are:

* scholarships, fellowships, prizes and awards
* brief mention of publications if it is inappropriate to mention them in a separate section
* fundraising for which you were responsible
* sporting successes.

Interests

It is a good idea to have at least a brief section on interests to show that you are not a one-dimensional person. The extent of this section depends on how you see its purpose in the overall CV. If there are plenty of relevant links between your qualifications and experience and the post for which you are applying, your interests section can be fairly brief. If possible, choose some interests which are complementary to the qualities required for the job. For example, If the job calls for highly developed social skills, don't list only solitary leisure pursuits.

When you have relatively little work experience and perhaps none which is directly related to the job which you want, you may have to elaborate rather more on your interests in order to identify personal characteristics which indicate the potential to cope with the demands of the job. In this case you may want to develop your interests section to demonstrate the transferable skills gained from these pursuits.

Example:

Tennis: I enjoy the competitive challenge of the sport as well as keeping fit. Last season I organised a programme of 'away' fixtures, including transport.

Skills profile

If you have highlighted skills throughout your CV, you may decide that this is sufficient. It can, however, be very effective to have a summary statement of skills drawn from all aspects of your experience towards the end of your CV. If you opt for this approach, focus very closely on the skills which you have identified as being on an employer's checklist. This is your chance to leave the reader with the impression that you fill the bill in every respect.

This is not the place for large blocks of text. The best layout is in bullet point format, as follows:

Skills profile

- Analytical skills   Ability to assess and interpret complex data and draw valid conclusions
- Written communication   Selection of appropriate forms of writing for instruction manuals, official correspondence and publicity for clients
- Negotiation skills   Construction of well founded negotiating positions, coupled with diplomacy and inter-personal skills.

Publications

This is an important section for an academic CV, but it is usually less important or even unnecessary for many other types of post. You can include here books, journal articles, papers published in conference proceedings and any other form of substantial professional writing. It is legitimate to include 'work in progress' if it is reasonably well advanced and does have a definite prospect of publication. You do not want to be accused of padding out your publications list with screeds of wishful thinking!

If the number of publications is fairly small, you may be able to include it in your CV, perhaps replacing one of the optional sections. If, however, the list is very long, it may be better to have it as an appendix so as not to unbalance the proportions of the CV. In that case you may want to make a cross-reference from a brief statement in the CV to the appendix (perhaps when describing your research).

Referees

It is normal to have at least two referees. For an academic post it is appropriate to have two academic referees. For most other posts it is better to have one academic and one work-related referee. If both of these would be academic, you may want to choose your current manager as one referee and find someone else who knows you in another capacity if you want employers to gain a perspective of you from outside the academic world. It goes without saying that you should ask permission of referees before naming them.

If you state details of your referees in full on your CV, give full addresses and telephone numbers. It is possible to state that references are available on request. This can delay the whole appointments process, but where there are good reasons for you not wishing your referees to be contacted unless you have a realistic chance of being appointed, this may be the best option.

If one or more of your referees happens to be overseas, there may be a disincentive for employers to entail delay in contacting them. To overcome that problem, you can ask such a referee to give you a testimonial. This is a written statement of how you performed in a previous post, with an assessment of your value as an employee and a recommendation from your previous employer to prospective recruiters.

Sample CVs

In order to be effective a CV must be relevant. The easiest way to understand the importance of this statement is to look at sample CVs and to decide which candidate you would select for a post.

Think back to Jill whom we met at the beginning of this chapter when she was preparing to apply for a post as a development officer with a local enterprise agency, working on fund-raising for and implementation of environmental improvement projects. You will remember that Jill reckoned that the post calls for the following competences:

- analytical ability
- creativity
- written communication
- oral communication
- forward planning
- organisation skills
- ability to monitor progress
- team work
- ability to handle finance
- fund-raising
- persuasive ability
- supervisory skills.

We shall soon see the CV which Jill prepared for this post, but first meet Hugh, one of the other candidates.

Hugh has some advantages over Jill, in that he comes originally from the area covered by the local enterprise agency and so has local knowledge. Unlike Jill, whose first degree was in geography, Hugh has a BA in landscape architecture before going on to take a higher degree in rural resource management. Seeing this post advertised, Hugh is keen to get his application in quickly. Surely the early bird will catch the worm? Fortunately, he has a ready-made CV (Figure 10.1), one which he used last month to apply for a lecturing post in Newcastle. Quick as a wink, he has it in the post and sits back to await his invitation to interview. Based on that CV, do you think he will be successful?

CURRICULUM VITAE

Name	Hugh Barnes Smith
Date of birth	3 September, 1969
Age	27
Marital status	Single
Address	2, The Stables Wynd
	Littlechester
	Cheshire, CH13 5YC
Tel	01234-772819

EDUCATION

1981–87 Newton Haven Grammar School

A level			O level				
Economics	A		Economics	A	Biology	A
Art	B		Art	A	French	B
Mathematics	B		Mathematics	A	English Language	B
			Physics	B	English Literature	C

1987–90   Tadcaster University
BA in Landscape Architecture (2.1 honours)

1990–92   University of Lincoln
M.Sc. in Rural Resource Management

1992–96   University of Chester
Ph.D. in Inward Investment as a Factor in the Development of Rural Resources
Using an econometric model of calculating the net value of investment by Government, international agencies and private investors in rural areas in England and Wales, I designed a comparative model to determine whether the value of the employment created in these areas and the consequent slowing of the rate of outward migration from the countryside by young people had a balancing effect on the stability and economic viability of these areas.
My calculations were done on a computer database designed by myself. This has numerous further applications for econometric modelling and I plan to use it in my future research.

WORK EXPERIENCE

Summers 1987–88   Catering assistant, Butlin's, Scarborough
Duties:- Keeping dining room tidy, preparing and serving meals

Summers 1989–90   Lee Carlton, Landscape Architects, Middlewich
Duties:- Initially, labouring on a land improvement project
Later, some design tasks in the main office

Summers 1991–92   Yellowstone National park, USA
Duties:- Initially, catering assistant in holiday lodges
Later, tour guide

1995–96   University of Chester, Department of Rural Management
Duties:- Tutorial assistant for groups of undergraduates

Figure 10.1 Hugh's CV (continued overleaf)

1996–present   University of Chester, Department of Rural Management
                    Duties:- Research assistant on project comparing rural
                            resource management in north-west England and
                            two other E.U. countries. This involves complex
                            econometric modelling and investigation of the
                            impact of environmental legislation on the pace of
                            development in each country.

PUBLICATIONS
C Harvey and H B Smith, 'Investing in the Rural Economy', in *British Journal of Rural Resource Management*, vol 6, 1996
H B Smith and L Leach, 'Economic Comparators in Rural Resource Management in England, Portugal and Sweden', in *Countryside*, vol 10, 1998

INTERESTS
Travelling, outdoor pursuits, home computing, good food

ADDITIONAL INFORMATION
Clean driving licence held since 1988
I am in excellent health

REFEREES
References are available on request.

Figure 10.1 (continued)

Assessment of Hugh's CV

What messages do you think Hugh got across to the selectors?

- He is very keen on computers and econometric modelling.
- He would like to do further research and seems keen on an academic career.
- He has limited relevant work experience.

When the selectors compare Hugh's CV with their checklist of criteria, many questions are left unanswered:

- Is he creative when left to his own initiative?
- Where is the evidence of his written and oral communication skills?
- When did he ever plan and organise a substantial event or activity?
- Does he work well in a team?

- There seems to be no evidence of budgeting or handling money, and yet that will be a core part of the job.
- Where is the evidence of fund-raising or making successful grant applications?
- Has he supervised people?
- He hasn't persuaded the selectors that he is the man for the job, so how could he succeed with other people?

The sad thing is that, had he given the application process more thought, Hugh had some good material to put into his CV, but he did not use it to best advantage.

- How did he manage to land the job at Yellowstone National Park? Did he use his initiative then?
- He has some publications, but has he written only in very academic journals? There must be other forms of writing he could cite.
- Surely he communicated with tourists in the Yellowstone National Park in a lively and entertaining way.
- Hugh is probably part of an international team of researchers and his work experience also suggests that he has been a team member on various occasions, but he has not spelled this out.
- Apart from minor cash handling in various jobs, Hugh must have access to a budget of some kind to conduct this international research project. As for fund-raising, how did he raise the money to go to America?
- The tutor–student relationship could be described as a supervisory role, but Hugh included it only as a throw away line.
- Working on a tripartite project is tricky, especially with three very different cultures involved. Surely Hugh has developed some persuasive and diplomatic skills through this experience?

Hugh will probably be quite surprised when he doesn't get an interview, but, nothing daunted, he will no doubt blow the dust off his CV and churn it out again as a countryside manager, a civil service research officer, a lecturer in landscape architecture and a tourist development officer in Cumbria. It is easy to see how some people can manufacture a continuous run of 'bad luck', isn't it?

Jill, with competition like this, you could be very successful!

Jill's CV

Let us now return to Jill and see how her careful preparatory work stands her in good stead as she compiles her CV (see Figure 10.2). She is clear about the messages which she has to deliver and about the evidence available to prove that she is a worthy candidate.

JILL HEMINGWAY
14, University Road
Aberdeen, AB2 4XZ
Tel: 01224-486733

CAREER GOAL   To apply my knowledge of environmental planning and enthusiastic commitment to practical conservation to a career in
environmental resource management, in a context which will
use my interpersonal and communication skills.

WORK EXPERIENCE

Environmental   Environmental research assistant, Department of Urban and
Regional Planning, University of Aberdeen, 1997–99 (fixed contract)
Jointly funded by the EU and Grampian Enterprise, our project
investigates the impact of incentives to farmers and landowners
to diversify the rural economy of north-east Scotland.

My responsibilities include:
* managing a budget of £15,000 [12% of the total]
* organising my own schedule and monitoring the progress of
  the project
* communicating with landowners and tenants via question-
  naires, one to one interviews and focus groups
* analysing statistical and other data
* presenting project findings in a written report and oral
  presentations.

Conservation volunteer, 1988–present
As a member of Student Conservation Groups and National
Trust for Scotland Conservation Working Parties, I have partici-
pated as a team member in conservation projects, including:
* restoration of buildings on St Kilda
* riverside clearance and path maintenance schemes
* reclaiming derelict urban land for recreation areas.

Tourism and   Elgin Tourist Board assistant, summers 1992–94
leisure   Aspects of the job which I particularly enjoyed were:
* advising tourists of attractions in the local area
* building working relationships with hoteliers, tour operators
  and members of the Tourist Board Committee

L'Hirondelle Summer Camp, Brittany, summer 1991
As one of a team of play leaders I was responsible for:

Figure 10.2 Jill's CV

- supervising children of several nationalities in groups of 30 at a time
- inspiring children to be enthusiastic about nature and wildlife
- organising a programme of activities in all weathers

EDUCATION

University of Aberdeen 1994–1997	Ph.D. in Environmental Planning Research topic: The role of the Forestry Commission in the economy of rural Scotland Benefits gained from my research included: • building a network of contacts in Government departments, LECs and nature and conservation agencies • developing my understanding of financial and statistical analysis
University of Strathclyde 1993–94	Diploma in Urban and Regional Planning Electives: Planning for Rural Communities Economic Aspects of Planning
University of St Andrews 1989–93	MA Honours (2.1) in Geography Dissertation: Land Use Regulations as a Tool for Conservation Subsidiary subjects: Economics and English

ACHIEVEMENTS

Two articles published in the British Journal of Rural Resource Management (1996–97)
Fife Medal awarded for Honours dissertation.
Member of group which raised £25,000 for National Trust for Scotland conservation projects.

INTERESTS

Conservation:	I am an active member of the NTS Conservation Volunteers
Gardening:	My aim is to transform a 'wilderness' allotment into a country garden
Sport:	Rowing and relay running are my favourite team sports
Arts:	For relaxation I enjoy theatre outings and concerts with friends.

SKILLS PROFILE

Communication	I communicate fluently with people at all levels and can address audiences at an appropriate level orally and in writing.
Project development	I can take a project from the creation of an initial concept though the planning stage to full implementation, including monitoring and cost control.
Interpersonal skills	Capable of working as a team member and a supervisor, I can motivate people and encourage harmonious working relationships.

Figure 10.2 (continued)

REFEREES

Professor J Williams, Department of Urban and Regional Planning, University of Aberdeen, AB24 4YQ
[Tel: 01224-467823]

Mrs N Stuart, National Trust for Scotland, 9 Charlotte Square, Edinburgh, EH1 7RT
[Tel: 0131-332-5548]

Figure 10.2 (continued)

Assessment of Jill's CV

Jill knew what messages she had to deliver in order to stand a chance of being interviewed and on the whole she has succeeded in what she set out to do. No CV is ever perfect, but at least Jill's has done her justice in a way which Hugh's did not.

- She has demonstrated both her academic knowledge of environmental issues and her personal commitment to the cause of conservation at a practical level.
- She uses vocabulary which suggests her creativity in contexts other than the writing of academic papers, phrases such as 'inspiring children' and 'transforming' her garden.
- Her versatility across a range of written and oral formats is displayed by citing examples.
- A powerful sentence on project development demonstrates her grasp of the process behind the successful completion of a project.
- Fundraising and financial capabilities are evidenced by facts about sums raised and managed.
- Vocabulary and examples suggesting good team work and supervisory experience are used in various contexts to demonstrate transferable skills.
- Several references to networks of contacts and the ability to relate well to people imply an ability to form the kinds of relationships which make it easier to negotiate with people in a 'win–win' situation.

Jill geared her CV for a non-academic post, but it would have looked substantially different had she applied for an academic post. In order to appreciate the contrast, let us return to Hugh, who having failed to gain an interview for the environmental development officer post, is now applying for a fixed term lecturing post in a university. How can he improve his CV to ensure selection for interview for an academic post? Compare the CV in Figure 10.3 with his first attempt (Figure 10.1).

HUGH BARNES SMITH
2, The Stables Wynd
Littlechester
Cheshire, CH13 5YC
Tel: 01234-772819
E-mail: h.b.smith@chester.ac.uk

EDUCATION

University of Chester
1992–96

Ph.D. in Inward Investment as a Factor in the Development of Rural Resources.

Synopsis attached. Key features included:-

- design of an econometric model to track correlations between inward investment and the growth of rural economies in England and Wales
- extensive use of databases and spreadsheets to manage and analyse complex statistics
- correspondence, surveys and interviews with representatives of local authorities, employers, Government departments and funding agencies.

University of Lincoln
1990–92

MSc in Rural Resource Management

- Electives included Environmental Impact Assessment and a work placement with the British Waterways Board
- Dissertation: The Economic Viability of Britain's Canals. This intensive study laid the foundation for my future work in econometrics.

Tadcaster University
1987–90

BA Honours (2.1) in Landscape Architecture

The syllabus provided a good balance of scientific, business and design subjects, with three work placements in the private and public sectors.

WORK EXPERIENCE

Academic

University of Chester
1996–present

Research assistant, Department of Rural Management

Member of a research team funded by the Natural Environmental Research Council in partnership with a local enterprise agency and the EU. Our comparative study of rural resource management in three countries involves complex econometric modelling and evaluation of the impact of environmental legislation on the development of rural economies.

1995–96

Tutorial assistant, Department of Rural Management

Following a course of instruction, I led seminars for undergraduates, marked essays and acted as a group leader on field trips.

Figure 10.3 Hugh's CV (2)

Environmental

Yellowstone National Park, USA 1991 and 1992	Tour guide
	To be effective as a tour guide, I had to assess the level of knowledge and interest of groups of visitors and tailor my interpretation of the reserve to suit their needs. This developed a lively style of appropriate communication.
Lee Carlton, Landscape Architects 1989–90	Design assistant and site labourer Experience here gave a good overview of landscaping projects, from design to implementation.

PUBLICATIONS

H B Smith and L Leach	'Economic Comparators in Rural Resource Management in England, Portugal and Sweden, in *Countryside*, vol 10, 1998
C Harvey and H B Smith	'Investing in the Rural Economy', in *British Journal of Rural Resource Management*, vol 6, 1996

Work in progress

H B Smith and L Leach	'Environmental Legislation for Protection and Development', to be published in *British Journal of Rural Resource Management*, vol 8, 1998

Conference proceedings

H B Smith	'Creating Incentives for Change', in *Proceedings of the 1997 Conference of the Association of Rural Resource Managers*, 1997

PROFESSIONAL AFFILIATIONS

Member of the Association of Rural Resource Managers
Secretary of the Cheshire branch of the British Rural Conservation Society

INTERESTS

Travel	Extensive journeys in Mediterranean, Nordic and North American countries
Outdoor pursuits	Orienteering, hill-walking and white water rafting for challenge and recreation
Computing	Exploration of the Internet for relaxation as well as research

Figure 10.3 (continued)

REFEREES

Prof C Harvey (Ph.D. Supervisor)
Dept of Rural Management
University of Chester
Castle Street
Chester, CH1 4LU
Tel: 01234-854321

Prof M Lawrence
President, Association of Rural
Resource Managers
School of Ecology
University of Falmouth
Cornwall, TR12 0PH
Tel: 01573-887664

Figure 10.3 (continued)

Assessment of Hugh's CV

The changes which Hugh has made in his CV are designed to emphasise his academic track record and make the most of those areas of his experience which may be considered rather lightweight. Note the following points in comparison with Hugh's first CV, and the difference in emphasis between Hugh's CV for an academic post and Jill's CV for a non-academic post.

- Hugh gives far greater prominence to his academic achievements, including details of techniques and methodologies and referring to an enclosed synopsis of his Ph.D. on a single page.
- He has omitted school qualifications as it is more important to devote space to his university courses.
- Hugh's background research on the vacant post told him that there is a social science rather than a business or scientific slant to the department's research and so he has emphasised the economics aspect of his studies, stressing how he made the transition from landscape architecture.
- While depth in a specialist subject is essential for a researcher, Hugh is aware that a certain degree of breadth is desirable for versatility as a lecturer to undergraduates, hence the explanation of the breadth of his BA course.
- Hugh's experience of tutoring undergraduates is relatively limited, but he has made the most of it by specifying various facets of his contact with students.
- Hugh's ability as an effective communicator, able to relate to audiences at various levels, is emphasised in his carefully selected explanation of the value of his tour guiding experience.
- Space is limited and so non-essential information, such as a post long ago as a catering assistant, has simply been omitted.
- The publications section has been expanded by including a published conference paper and an article currently in progress (legitimate as it has been accepted for publication, subject to minor amendments).

- There is less emphasis on transferable skills than in Jill's CV because subject knowledge is of more significance, but the section on interests shows that Hugh is not a one-dimensional person.
- Both referees are academics, appropriate for this post, but not necessarily the best combination had Hugh applied for a non-academic post.

Covering letters

To complete her application Jill needs an effective covering letter. Before looking at her version, let us consider the key components of any covering letter. A simple model which can be adapted for most purposes contains three sections. The same principles apply to Hugh's covering letter for an academic post.

Introduction

Tell the selector why, out of all the jobs in the world, this one appeals to you and has prompted your application.

- It may relate directly to your academic work.
- It may have a connection with a life-long interest such as Jill's commitment to conservation.
- It may give you opportunities at a senior level in a field in which your current job has given you relevant experience.

After reading this opening paragraph, the selector should feel that this is not a random application, but one which has received serious thought because of a substantial area of common interest between you and the organisation advertising the vacancy.

Highlight your assets

Having said why you are interested in the job, now tell the selectors why they should be interested in you. Here you will give them 'la creme de la CV', your three or four most relevant selling points for this post.

Without repeating large chunks of the CV verbatim, highlight your strongest attributes and underpin them with concise evidence; for example:

'My contribution to this post will draw upon the following attributes:

- Building design experience for major clients, including the University of Silchester and the National Forestry Commission
- Supervisory skills, developed in practical settings on building sites and in an academic context while supervising undergraduate dissertations.'

14, University Road
Aberdeen, AB2 4XZ

Ms. M. Harvey,
Personnel Officer,
Cumbria Enterprise Agency,   15 May, 1999
Denvent Street,
Barrow-in-Furness, CR22 4ZB

Dear Ms. Harvey,

Environmental development officer
[Ref. EDO/WCEA/19/99]

I wish to express my keen interest in the post of environmental development officer, which was advertised in 'The Guardian' on 8 May, 1999. The post provides an ideal opportunity to combine my interest in environmental issues with a remit for positive, practical action in a setting which would use my talent for effective interaction with people at all levels, from E.U. officials to members of the community.

At this stage in my career I can offer a combination of knowledge, experience and personal attributes which would enable me to perform this role to your satisfaction. In particular, I would highlight:-

• my understanding of the priorities and funding criteria of the E.U. and enterprise agencies, developed through partnership with them in the evaluation of grant aided projects for the rural economy;
• experience of managing complex projects to a successful conclusion within the required time-scales;
• a good intellectual grasp of environmental issues, coupled with extensive practical experience of conservation, involving team work with professionals and volunteers.

I shall be pleased to supply further information on any aspect of the experience and qualifications outlined in my CV. I look forward to the opportunity to discuss the advertised post and my application at either a formal interview or an informal discussion.

Yours sincerely,

(Dr) Jill Hemingway

Figure 10.4 Sample covering letter

Positive conclusion

Maintain a confident awareness of your own value in the concluding paragraph by suggesting that there will be mutual benefit in progressing this application to the next stage. You can do this by offering to supply further information, inviting contact with your referees, or indicating your eagerness to discuss your application at an informal discussion or a formal interview.

If the covering letter is part of a speculative application, you may wish to indicate that you will follow up with a 'phone call within the next fortnight to see if your application is of interest to the organisation concerned.

Let us now return to Jill to see how she applies this model to her covering letter (Figure 10.4).

Assessment of Jill's covering letter

- The selector is left in no doubt about Jill's enthusiasm for this post. The obvious relevance of the post to her qualifications and experience lend assurance that this is not simply one of a batch of assorted applications for all kinds of jobs.
- In the crucial middle paragraph Jill has chosen very carefully the order in which she mentions her best selling points. This is certainly a post where knowledge of environmental issues is important, but primarily it is a development officer's job. The selectors therefore do not want someone who will have no interest in the practical issues of applying for grants and achieving projects on time and to the specified standards. Jill indicates that she understands the frame of reference in which she will be working and the importance of building good relationships with key players. Note how she uses words such as 'partnership', 'evaluation', 'practical experience' and 'team work' to create the image which her background research has told her will match the selectors' criteria.
- The positive note at the end of the letter sounds as if Jill is confident that what she has to offer will merit entry to the next stage of selection: the interview!

In chapter 12 we shall follow the selection process through to the interview stage, but first let us consider how the techniques for effective presentation of CVs can be applied to situations where the first stage of selection is via an application form.

Chapter 11

Application forms

While selection in many countries is primarily via CVs, the British have a peculiar attachment to that leveller of candidates, the application form. Introduced originally to give all applicants an equal opportunity to present themselves well, it is regarded by many as a straitjacket which confines applicants to answering questions which in many instances they would rather ignore. Readers of this book may find themselves applying primarily via CVs, but it is as well to be prepared for the different challenges posed by application forms.

There are, broadly speaking, two categories of application form: the deceptively simple and the evidently searching. Most of our time in this chapter will be spent on the latter, but it is worth saying a few words about the former, which have been known to bowl out the unwary.

Simple application forms

Some organisations use a very basic form which is little more than an initial screening and recording device for applicants for all manner of posts from manual jobs through to chief executive. For more senior posts such a form alone is likely to give an inadequate representation of what candidates have to offer.

The general rule of thumb in such a situation is that if you genuinely feel that vital information is lacking without which you are not fairly represented, it may be advisable to attach a CV to the form, unless this is expressly forbidden in the application instructions.

This advice does not give you *carte blanche* to ride roughshod over all manner of applications by routinely enclosing CVs. This strategy should be adopted only where a CV is explicitly or implicitly required to demonstrate your relevant qualities, skills and experience in addition to the very basic facts covered on the application form.

Complex application forms

Most application forms are more demanding, and not all are well designed or even relevant to the range of posts for which they are used. Before putting a single word on the page, it is as well to step back and consider what application forms are intended to do.

- Application forms should allow candidates to present themselves in the best possible light for a particular post. Thus, although a question may be phrased in a general way, with application to many posts, it should always be answered with reference to the particular post for which a candidate is applying. (Examples are given below.)
- Application forms invite candidates to provide evidence of their suitability for a post. There is no place for sweeping generalisations or vague claims. Statements of a candidate's suitability should be backed up by relevant facts, which will stand up to further investigation at an interview.
- The application form is the script for the interview. A wise candidate can sow seeds for discussion by choosing examples and introducing topics which selectors will want to pick up in the interview. The more areas of common interest that are mentioned in the application, the more likely it is that the candidate will be able to forecast a large proportion of what will be discussed in the interview.

As in other disciplines, theories of personnel selection are not static and application form design reflects different schools of thought on what selectors should try to find out about candidates. It may help you as a candidate to understand some of the basic principles behind selection in order to appreciate the rationale behind application forms.

Theoretically, selection should begin with the production of a job description and a person specification.

- The job description states the duties and responsibilities of the post and the tasks which require to be undertaken in order that these should be discharged.
- The person specification indicates the qualifications, skills, experience and personal attributes required of the ideal candidate for the optimum performance of the job. Sometimes these items are divided into essential requirements without which candidates will not be short-listed, and desirable attributes which will help selectors to decide on a short-list if there is a particularly strong field of candidates.

In this context, the application form is a vehicle by which candidates supply, and selectors identify, evidence that applicants possess all of the essential and as many as possible of the desirable requirements for the vacant post. In the ideal world, each application form would be tailor-made to suit each vacancy, but in reality organisations' application forms are normally issued for many types of post and it is therefore left to the applicant to customise the answers to suit a particular position.

Some types of application forms, and hints for answers

Competences

A very obvious way of comparing applicants with the person specification is to ask them to give evidence of their possession of the competences required for the post. This is often elicited in the form of a description of situations in which the applicant has demonstrated certain skills or qualities, for example:

- Describe a situation where you have had to influence a group of people to accept your proposal. How did you convince them?
- Describe a situation where you had to overcome an obstacle or a serious disappointment. How did you motivate yourself to continue?

The main pitfall to be avoided here is a lapse into unthinking narrative which makes few cogent points about your characteristics and skills. Indeed, in approaching such an application form do not immediately start raking around in your memory for incidents to describe. Go back to the person specification and think of all the competences which you will try to demonstrate via this form. Then plan out which competences you will demonstrate in answer to each question. Only then begin to think of situations which will act as vehicles for conveying to selectors your possession of the necessary requirements for the job.

In constructing your answer to such questions, set the scene briefly, but devote the second half of the answer to demonstrating the skills and qualities which you used or developed through the incident, including any learning which you gained as a result. In this way even a situation which had negative overtones can be used to demonstrate personal growth.

Remember that selectors use the application form as a vehicle to find out about you as an individual. Therefore in questions about situations involving team-work, indicate the individual contribution which you made to the team effort, not necessarily as a leader, but as an encourager, a creative spirit or whatever you feel your personal style to be.

Biodata

Some forms or sections of forms are very highly structured and ask you simply to tick boxes or otherwise indicate basic data about your age, qualifications and practical skills. Such forms are often used in a first sift to sort out candidates who are eligible from those who patently are not. These are not usually difficult to complete, but they can engender an anxiety about being misunderstood in applicants who have the feeling that they fall outside 'the norm'. If, for instance, you are an older candidate or have entered university through a non-traditional route and therefore do not fit the standard pattern of school leaving qualifications, you may feel that you will fall at the first hurdle if application forms are treated in a mechanistic way.

At the end of the day if an organisation does not use discretion in reviewing such forms, candidates who are even a little 'unorthodox' may be ruled out, but credit has to be given to most organisations for not operating in quite such a cut and dried fashion. If, therefore, you feel that an explanation is required – for instance, for not having 'A' level or Higher grades – make a brief mention of this on the form at the appropriate place with a cross reference to a covering letter or an additional sheet of notes. It is important to make a note on the form as a separate sheet or a letter can be detached from a form during processing. Another tactic is to discuss the point at issue with a selector on the telephone and to make reference to the conversation on the form and/or covering letter.

Such tactics are advisable if there are only a few points in the form which you feel may be misunderstood. If, however, you have the feeling that the profile being suggested by the format of the application form has very little in common with your own, it may be wise to reconsider whether an application to this organisation is likely to be successful. It can be hard to change selectors' view of what they want, and your talents may be better appreciated elsewhere.

Electronic scanning

Some organisations – particularly those in the high technology sector – either accept applications over the Internet or, on receiving paper applications, scan these electronically at the first stage of selection. Further advice on electronic applications is given in the *Guide to Job Search via the Internet for Academic Researchers*, but a few key points are given below.

Instructions are often given as to the key selection criteria which should be mentioned in the application form, but if not, then it is a good idea to ring and ask about this before completing the application form. Otherwise, you could be unfairly screened out because you did not mention key facts which the scanner is programmed to identify on applications.

These factors vary from one organisation to another and it is therefore important to find out as much as possible about the organisation's activities and selection criteria. For instance, it may not be sufficient to say that you are computer literate if the scanner is primed to look for details of specific computer languages. Likewise, vocabulary indicating teamwork, leadership or entrepreneurial skills may trigger selection.

Classic questions on applications

It is dangerous to look for formula answers to questions on application forms. What distinguishes successful candidates is the freshness of their language and the originality of their approach to answering questions. Nonetheless, it is impossible to gauge the nature of your response if you do not understand the purpose of particular questions. The rest of this chapter is devoted to demystifying some classic types of questions and indicating what kind of response is helpful to selectors.

Questions on academic qualifications

If you have several qualifications, this section of an application form may be inadequate. If the form allows you to select the main qualifications, highlight aspects which are relevant to the job, for instance, choosing to mention an elective on photosynthesis if this seems pertinent to the vacant post, but not some others. On the other hand, if the form wants all qualifications from school onwards, state the main qualifications on the form and give specific details on an enclosed sheet, which should be mentioned in a cross-reference on the form and firmly stapled to the form, with your name written at the top of the page as a further safeguard should it become detached.

If there are questions about what you have gained from your education, do not answer these in a vacuum, but be conscious of the requirements of the job for which you are applying. There is little point, for instance, in mentioning how much you enjoyed a three-month period of isolation, studying gulls' eggs on a rocky outcrop if the job is going to involve constant negotiation and interaction with people!

Questions on work experience

The emphasis here is usually on the competences, knowledge and techniques which you have gained and which could be transferred into a different context. In tackling such a question, you have to assess how much vocabulary and common knowledge is shared between yourself and the selectors. You also have to take into account whether the post for which you are applying is in the same field that you are in at present or whether you are attempting to make a fairly radical switch from one function or sector to another.

If it is a fair assumption that there is a large area of common understanding between yourself and the selectors, you need not spell out every acronym or abbreviation which is well known in your profession. Likewise, if you are applying within your own sector or function you may not have to spell out what certain aspects of your work entail, although be sure that you do not undersell yourself if the scale, originality or complexity of your work exceeds the norm.

On the other hand, if you think you will be addressing selectors who may be less familiar with your area of experience or type of academic background, you may have to act as an interpreter, spelling out to them the relevance of the skills and knowledge which you have gained to the post which they seek to fill. Avoid the jargon of your profession which is not likely to be well understood by people outside your field.

Questions relating to achievements

The purpose of such questions is not to see if you are in the super-league, but to tell selectors how closely your account of your successes match what they will require you to do in a job. In approaching such a question you should therefore go back again to the fundamental starting point: what do they want you to be able to do?

Although you cannot manufacture achievements to suit all circumstances, nonetheless you should look for a success story in your life which will amply demonstrate what you want to prove about yourself in relation to the post for which you are applying. For instance, if you are applying for an academic post, you will almost certainly want to cite an academic achievement such as a scholarship won against strong competition, a research grant achieved against difficult odds or a project outcome which exceeded sponsors' expectations.

On the other hand if you are applying for a post in a non-research capacity outside higher education, too strong an emphasis on academic achievements might merely confirm an impression that academia is your natural milieu and you might be out of place elsewhere. Depending on the nature of the post sought, you may want to highlight a fund-raising campaign in order to demonstrate your entrepreneurial flair or a situation requiring diplomacy or the motivation of yourself and others against competition or adversity if you can expect to encounter such situations in your future employment.

Questions on landmarks in your life

These questions may ask about major influences in your career or may simply confront you with a dauntingly large blank sheet and an invitation to fill it with significant events from babyhood to the present day. This type of question may appear to have little connection with the job for which you are applying, but remember that the selectors' agenda does not change throughout the selection process. They are constantly looking for evidence that your profile matches as closely as possible that of their ideal candidate.

Viewed in that context, this type of question is simply another opportunity for you to demonstrate that you possess attributes which your new employers would prize. You should therefore select your landmarks with a view to showing these traits or how you acquired knowledge which is pertinent to the vacant post. While the specific factors will vary from post to post, it is worth making some general points about this type of question.

- If the space for the answer is large, create a framework for yourself and break points for the reader's eye by dividing the page into sections with headings and indentations of key points. Reading the question carefully to ensure that you cover all the elements in it will help you to see what the structure should be.
- Selectors are always interested in how people cope with turning points in

their lives, when important decisions had to be made and they base conclusions about future performance on the patterns which they perceive in the past. They will want to know if you appear to drift into the easy option or take the line of least resistance or whether you weigh up all the pros and cons and sometimes choose a difficult path which will be beneficial in the long run. Are you overly influenced by others, or do you take soundings appropriately and then reach your own well considered decision?

- There is no obligation to pretend that you have had the wisdom of Solomon from the age of five. It is good to show that you have reflected on and learned from situations which may have been difficult, disappointing or distressing at the time. The ability to overcome obstacles and surmount problems and come through them as a stronger, wiser person is a quality which employers value.
- Do not make mountains out of molehills, or vice versa. It is counterproductive to over-elaborate on the benefits of a fairly mundane activity. For instance, there is a limit as to how much one can emphasise the level of communication skills gained from a spell as a waitress. More commonly, however, applicants undersell their achievements. For example, there is no need to sound apologetic about having a 2.2 degree if it was gained in conjunction with holding down a substantial part-time job, commuting daily and maintaining family responsibilities. The points to stress in such a situation would be the versatility, stamina and time-management skills developed in keeping such a hectic life-style under control.

Questions on your contribution to the new post

This question requires you to gain as good a grasp as you can of the organisation – its mission, priorities and operations. Literature outlining these may be supplied with the job description, but in other cases you may have to research via annual reports, Web home pages and informal conversations with people who are familiar with the organisation. If possible, try to find out how the post for which you are applying fits into the overall picture.

Once you have this background information, questions about your contribution become easier to answer. How can your knowledge, talents and skills be harnessed to help the organisation to do what it wants to do? The more bridges you can build between their needs and your contribution, the more likely it is that you will be the successful candidate.

Techniques for handling other questions

It is impossible to cover all potential problem questions. What causes one person difficulty may be straightforward for another. In general, the following strategies will help you to make a good attempt at most questions.

- Ask yourself, 'What is the purpose of this question in relation to the job?' If you cannot work that out, try asking someone who is familiar with application forms, such as a careers adviser or a personnel officer. Failing that, even a second opinion from a friend may throw a different perspective on the question for you.
- Be guided by the over-riding principle that the whole application is a series of opportunities for you to present evidence of your understanding of what is required in the post and your suitability to fill it.
- Pay as much attention to the structure and layout of your answers as to the content.
- The best answer can be negated if it is illegible or gives an impression of untidiness or scant attention to detail. It is a good idea to have a trial run on a photocopy of the application, which allows you to edit it down to the essentials if lack of space is a problem.

If the post is appropriate and if you follow these guidelines, you should soon be able to move on to preparing for an interview. Chapter 12 will show you what is required.

Chapter 12

Convincing selectors
Interviews

Notification of an interview should be cause for celebration, but so often the first impulse of gladness is rapidly replaced by a sense of anxiety and fear of being unable to cope with whatever the interviewers may ask. While a touch of adrenalin can add sparkle to one's performance, a surfeit can lead to disaster. This chapter will help you to understand the purpose and format of interviews and so replace a feeling of dread with one of confident anticipation.

The purpose of interviews

Whether you are being interviewed for an academic or a non-academic post, the purpose of an interview remains the same. To have reached an interview you must have shown that on paper you are an acceptable candidate. In the interview the selectors will therefore explore whether:

- all that you have claimed on paper is borne out in reality
- some candidates have more to offer than others when pressed beyond the point of the limited amount of information on an application form
- there is good 'personal chemistry' between you as a candidate and the people with whom you will be working; in other words, will you fit into the organisation.

Some of the information which selectors seek to gather at interviews is tangible and can be demonstrated beyond a shadow of a doubt. For instance, you either can or cannot do C++ programming, and if need be that aptitude can be tested.

Much of the territory covered in an interview, however, rests on perception and so the image which you convey and the interpretation which you encourage the selectors to place upon the facts which you present are absolutely vital to the outcome of the interview. Of course, a positive attitude on your part may not overcome the predilection of a panel who are bent on appointing a preferred candidate, but you can be sure that signs of a negative, defeatist or truculent attitude will scupper your prospects, even if on paper you have been the front runner, and interviews are a contest in which front runners frequently do not win!

The importance of the interviewee's attitude underlines the fact that interviewees can have much more control in an interview than they might imagine to be possible. It is therefore with the building of a positive attitude that you should begin your preparation for an interview.

Preparing for interviews

If ever preparation were nine-tenths of the battle, then interviews are a case in point. By the time you reach the interview, you want to glide across the surface like a swan, but meanwhile, below the surface the feet have been paddling industriously for some time. Your preparation should cover the following points:

- cultivating a positive frame of mind
- researching the organisation
- researching the job
- preparing for obvious and difficult questions
- creating the right visual image.

Positive thinking

Some people seem to be blessed with a positive outlook from the cradle onwards, whereas others have a natural talent for seeing the potential difficulties and draw-backs in a situation. The latter trait is not without its advantages in some situations, but selection interviews rarely come into that category. Whether or not you are one of nature's Pollyannas with an in-built tendency to be resilient and look on the bright side, it is possible for most people to coach themselves into a positive frame of mind for an interview. If you find that impossible in a given instance, you should seriously question whether to take up everybody's time by going along to an interview with a negative attitude or a feeling that defeat is assured, as that will almost certainly become a self-fulfilling prophecy.

In order to bolster your optimism, take yourself through the following train of thought:

- Since you have been invited to interview, it is a fair assumption that on paper you appear to be capable of doing the job. Busy selectors do not have time to interview 'non-starter' candidates. They are not interviewing you to pass the time of day. Had no candidates been suitable, they would have re-advertised the post.
- The volume of applications received varies greatly from post to post, but in many instances the fact that you have been called for interview means that you were among the top 5 or 10 per cent of all applicants. It is therefore an achievement to have reached this far in the process.
- The selectors obviously like what they have read about you so far. This tells you two useful facts. First, that the selectors are favourably disposed toward

you and hope that you will live up to the paper image which they have of you. Second, they are bound to want to talk about some of the things that they have read about you. Since you wrote the application form or CV (and kept a copy!), you therefore also have the script for at least part of the interview, which makes it less of an unknown quantity.

- At this stage – or at any stage – it is not worth worrying or even thinking about the other candidates. Whatever their merits or de-merits may be, these are beyond your influence. The only thing which is within your control is your own performance, and this requires your total concentration.
- Confront the worst-case scenario in advance of the interview, and you will find that it is not the end of the world. Probably the most disconcerting thing that can happen is that you may be asked a question to which you do not know the answer. If handled correctly, this need not be fatal to your prospects, unless, of course, it is elementary! Later in this chapter we shall look at techniques for handling difficult situations which may arise in interviews.
- Do not underestimate the value of physical exercises when trying to develop a relaxed mind in a relaxed body. Deep breathing, tensing and relaxing various sets of muscles, taking fresh air and exercise prior to an interview, all of these tactics can help to ensure that your body isn't working against your mind when it needs to be in perfect condition to let you be on your best form.

Researching the organisation

You should have done some research on your potential future employer before making an application, but now you need to increase your efforts to find out as much as you can about the institution or organisation to which you are applying. This is easier for large than for small organisations, but the principles are the same within the limits of what it may be possible to discover about the following issues.

- How does the institution or organisation perceive itself? For example, as an established market leader, a niche player or a fast rising star?
- What is its mission, and is this changing or developing from what it used to be?
- What signals does the organisation send out about its culture? For instance, is it hierarchical or democratic, centralised or devolved, formal or informal, nurturing or competitive? The clue is in the adjectives which it uses to describe itself.
- What are the big issues for the organisation, currently and in the future? For example, are there plans for de-layering the staffing structure? Is it in a sector where mergers are taking place? Are there international events or trends which are having an impact on the organisation, or are there global factors such as environmental issues which will change the way it operates?
- How is the organisation's business faring, whether it be an institution winning research contracts or a commercial concern increasing export sales and taking out patents on new products?

You may not be able to find out all of this information, but in piecing together as much as you can, you will be at least as well informed as other candidates or, more likely, ahead of the field. Sources which you can use include annual reports, staff magazines, faculty handbooks, World Wide Web home pages, product manuals and a range of business information services (such as Extel and Reuters) which are available in academic and business libraries.

What you are seeking to do with such information is not to be able to repeat it verbatim or to clog your brain with more data than you can usefully manage. The purpose is to ensure that you have a good general impression of the organisation which you claim to be so eager to join and that you will not be tripped up by being unaware of issues which the selectors consider to be essential to an understanding of the company or institution. This background knowledge will also help you to set in its proper context the job for which you are being interviewed.

Researching the job

As with the organisation, so too with the job the time has come for further preparation. If you have been given a contact to phone for further information, be sure to do so as otherwise that is a lost opportunity, but think carefully in advance about what you want to ask as you do not want to appear either vague or over-inquisitive. Failing a contact within the organisation, you may be able to find someone else who knows about this line of work via friends, relatives, former colleagues, a careers service or an alumni office.

You may want to know the following kinds of information at this stage.

- What is the line of management above and below this post?
- What proportions of time are allocated to various aspects of the job? (This may indicate which aspects of your experience the interviewers will probe most.)
- Where does budgetary responsibility lie?
- What are the arrangements – if any – for support services for this post?

To this list you can add further questions which will enable you to know which elements of your knowledge and experience you should emphasise at the interview.

Preparing for obvious and difficult questions

Inevitably there will be some questions at the interview which you could not have predicted, but, as with examinations, most of the hard work should have been done before you reach the interview room.

Some questions are so obvious that they underlie the whole interview and are bound to be asked in one way or another. Think in advance therefore about how you will tackle the following obvious questions.

What is the appeal of this job?

This is where you can use your knowledge of the organisation and the post to good advantage to indicate the attractions for you. This question also gives you an opportunity to begin to highlight your relevant skills and knowledge, thus reinforcing the selectors' impression of your suitability for the post. For example:

'I would enjoy this post because it would allow me to use my . . . and further develop my . . .'

Why do you wish to leave your current job?

Why do you want to make a career move at this stage?

Having explored the 'pull' factors in the previous question, the selectors are now investigating the 'push' factors. If the new post is offering you career development, a fresh start in a new field, a higher salary, more security, or an opportunity to continue your research, you can be very positive about your reply. What you want to avoid is a litany of complaint against your current employers which may suggest that you would not be long in finding cause for grievance in your new situation.

What can you bring to this post?

What can you contribute to this organisation/research team?

Here you can draw on and expand upon the information which you successfully conveyed in the application which secured you a place in the short list, but this is not an invitation to indulge in a twenty-minute monologue. Think in advance about which 'selling points' are most relevant when you are presented with this opportunity to state your case in person. If in the interval since applying you have found out more about the post, you may wish to change the emphasis slightly in your verbal reply to reinforce factors which perhaps were not so prominent in your written application.

How would you describe your strengths and weaknesses?

Although not always asked openly, this question is implicit in any interview. It should be answered, not in the abstract, but in the context of the post for which you are applying. Mention strengths which support your claim to be suitable for the post. For example:

'My ability to . . . would be beneficial in respect of . . . aspect of this post.'

Likewise, with weaknesses avoid mentioning anything which would be detrimental to the performance of the new job. You may choose to mention something which has little bearing on the job or indicate that a certain activity is not an area of natural strength for you, but one where you are now confident about your performance through persevering in order to improve. For example:

> 'Making presentations to large groups used to terrify me, but since undertaking training, I now find that I receive positive feedback about my presentation style.'

Other predictable questions

Looking back at the application form, job description and person specification, you should be able to predict issues which are liable to come up at the interview. Take time to prepare answers and if possible, rehearse them with someone who can give you honest feedback.

Questions which you don't want to answer

If you think, 'I do hope that they don't ask me about . . .', that is the very question which you should prepare to answer. The chances are that if it occurs to you, it may well occur to the interviewers. It is far better to work out a logical answer in advance than to hope against hope that the question will not arise, and then be floored when it does.

What you regard as difficult depends on your circumstances and temperament, and so it is impossible to cover here all the difficult questions which may arise, but comments on some perceived problem areas may be helpful.

Spells of unemployment

The fact that you were not in paid employment does not mean that you were doing nothing. You may have been doing voluntary work, engaged in preparing research grant applications, furthering your knowledge through formal or informal study, travelling or recovering from an illness or injury. Any of these occupations can be presented in a positive way. What does not go down well is the statement that you were applying for jobs. This may be so, but it does not sound like a full-time occupation, and do you really want to draw attention to the fact that this was your 112th application?

Age

Universities tend not to be against age in their outlook as they are accustomed to people making a late start in academic life. The Civil Service and the public sector in general also tend to be fairly relaxed about age on entry. Unfortunately, however, you may sometimes encounter either individuals or whole organisations with narrow views about age in relation to employment. If you have won through to an interview, you must conclude that your age is not perceived as an insuperable barrier, but you may nonetheless have to work harder than the other candidates to persuade selectors to appoint you.

If the selectors are inclined to think that you are too old for the post, you may have to produce evidence to convince them that:

- you fit in well with team members of all ages, including managers who are younger than you
- your maturity enables you to cope well with situations calling for diplomacy and sensitivity in dealing with people
- the diversity in your background brings extra perspectives to your work
- a later career change makes it less likely that you will move or take a career break.

If selectors had had someone older than you in mind for the post, you need to convince them that:

- there is good evidence of your potential to develop into this role even if you have not had directly similar experience
- you can demonstrate other examples of being able to cope with a fast learning curve
- your character is mature even if your chronological age is young
- you would not have a problem about being in charge of older people, even if it was a new experience for them.

Disability

If you have a disability of some kind, your main aim during an interview will be to keep the focus on your ability to perform the duties of the post as well as, if not better than, other candidates. None the less, the issue of coping with certain aspects of the job may arise. Selectors may not discriminate against you on the grounds of a disability, but they are entitled to ask about practical matters relating to the job. Your pre-interview research should therefore include investigation of any special measures which would enable you to do the job as well as any other candidate.

Points which may arise in an interview are listed below. Remember that the selectors may not know all the answers and may look to you for guidance to some extent. Do not be overly critical of their lack of knowledge as long as their attitude is positive and helpful.

- Be prepared to explain how you cope in your present employment by the use of equipment, auxiliaries or re-organisation of work routines to suit your needs.

- Cite performance indicators which demonstrate both the volume and quality of your output. Beware, however, of setting up for yourself targets which you cannot possibly meet.
- You may need to clarify the difference between having a disability and a poor absence record through illness.
- Clarify access arrangements and be conversant with assistance which employers can receive in adapting premises and installing equipment.

Moving across or down

Despite the widespread 'de-layering' of the work-force, some selectors still want to probe a candidate's proposed 'down-shifting' or lateral move. If you are in such a position, you need to be very clear about your own motivation and able to explain it logically at interview. There are numerous sensible reasons why you may want to make such a move.

- In seeking a fresh start in a new field you may have to be prepared to go in at the bottom of the ladder – possibly taking a drop in salary – because your experience may not be directly relevant. You may consider this to be worthwhile because of your interest in that area of work and the better long-term prospects.
- At a certain stage in your career you may have other priorities apart from fast acceleration along the career track, for instance, if you need a job which has flexible working hours, is part-time or does not involve you in evening work or extensive travel.
- You may want to step out of a pressurised post for health reasons or in order to complete part-time study or to begin to develop your own business on a part-time basis, although in some of these instances you will have to be careful that selectors will not conclude that you may have divided loyalties.
- You may be satisfied with a job which has better security and a regular income as opposed to one where short contracts come in fits and starts, or not at all.

Creating the right visual image

At one time advice on appearance at interviews was simple: get a suit and polish your shoes. Today more subtlety has crept into your visual image and this is usually taken to include your body language as well as what you wear.

Dress

Your background research on the organisation should give you a clue as to how formal or informal it is on a day to day basis. For an interview it is safe to err on the side of greater formality than on an average day, but even so this is relative to the style of the organisation and the format of the interview. If you are going for an informal chat in a laboratory office, it may be over the top to go along in a very formal suit. On the other hand, appearing in trainers at a formal panel interview may be regarded as a breach of the acceptable dress code.

Within the context of what you have found out about the institution or organisation, the following general comments on dress at interviews may be helpful.

- Your aim at interview should be for your appearance to be noted initially as being smart and appropriate, and then forgotten as the interviewers concentrate on what you are saying.
- An interview is rarely the place to make an idiosyncratic statement about yourself through your clothes. A certain degree of conformity may be necessary, even if you will not be required to come to work in a suit every day.
- Wear something which is comfortable, even if it is borrowed! You cannot afford to have your concentration distracted by the discomfort of a tight waistband or shoes which pinch.
- Smart trouser suits for women are acceptable in virtually all organisations, whereas attempts at 'power-dressing' are usually considered in bad taste, even if you could afford it!

Body language

Psychologists tell us that a large proportion of the impression which we have on others is created by non-verbal signals rather than the spoken word. Furthermore, if there is a conflict between these two forms of communication, it is our body language and not our words which are believed by observers.

For instance, if we feign enthusiasm in words which are accompanied by a limp body, an unsmiling face, and a flat tone, selectors will not be convinced. Likewise, poor eye contact and nervous mannerisms do not augur well for a candidate who will be expected to exude confidence on first acquaintance with strangers.

It is not necessary, however, to become neurotic about every movement in an interview as a candidate who sits stock-still is also very disconcerting to interviewers. The basic rule of appropriate body language is to be natural and relaxed. The following comments may help.

- Posture can say a great deal about a person's confidence and energy levels. Good, upright posture also helps with correct breathing patterns, which in turn supply oxygen to the brain when it needs to be on the alert.
- Sitting well back in your chair with your hands resting gently on your lap is a good position in which to begin an interview. When well supported, your back and shoulders can release any tension and you are in a good position to turn from side to side if there is a panel of interviewers.
- A genuine smile can help an interview along. Think about how fortunate

you are to be at this interview and how glad you are to meet the interviewers. Smiles from one party tend to generate smiles from others and so the tone of the interview becomes lighter.

- Only non-relevant, repetitive gestures are classed as fidgeting. Some gestures reinforce speech and are quite apt. For instance, an encompassing sweep of the hands to indicate wholeness or completion will probably be scarcely noticed by selectors as it is an integral part of the meaning of the speaker's words.

Formats of interviews

Part of the process of preparation involves understanding the dynamics of different kinds of interviews which you may encounter. As far as possible, you want to avoid being thrown off balance by walking into an unexpected situation. If the format of the interview is not declared in advance, it is not unreasonable to call and ask what form it will take. Some common forms of interviews are described in this section.

Group interviews

Group interviews may be used as an initial form of screening where there is a very large number of suitable candidates and it is difficult to draw up a short-list for one to one or panel interviews. It is more likely that this form of first interview will be used for posts which call for a considerable amount of interaction with people and working in groups.

In such a setting, selectors would be wary of people who:

- tried to dominate the conversation
- tried to up-stage others
- contributed little or nothing to the discussion
- were too aggressive or controversial
- appeared to have no opinions of their own
- went off at tangents unrelated to the main flow of the discussion
- cut across other people's conversation.

Conversely, the following kinds of behaviour would be considered constructive:

- listening to others and building on what they have said
- acknowledging the contributions of others
- referring back to points raised by others earlier in the conversation
- addressing or referring to others by name
- being courteously tentative rather than obstinately dogmatic
- inviting the opinions of others, especially quieter members of the group
- bringing the conversation back round to the relevant points for discussion
- summarising at appropriate stages in the discussion
- encouraging consensus, drawing on all the useful ideas which have emerged.

Informal one to one discussion

It might be said that if selection is on the agenda, there is no such thing as an informal discussion, as selectors' views of candidates are being formed from the minute that they meet. Nonetheless, conversations do take place outside of a formal interview setting if, for instance, you are invited to call and see the place where you would be working or to find out more about a post before deciding whether to apply.

In this situation you could damage your prospects by:

- not being organised about what you want to ask
- appearing to be lacking in curiosity: having very few questions to ask
- being over-inquisitive: asking insensitive or trivial questions
- being high-handed with staff other than those you consider to be important
- being too relaxed and naïve about what you say about your own experience and characteristics
- being too frank and critical about either the organisation you are leaving, or the one you seek to join.

On the other hand, you can score extra points by:

- planning in advance what you want to ask
- being clear about your own selling points which you want to introduce –subtly! – even at this early stage
- demonstrating some knowledge about the organisation, but taking the opportunity to find out more
- displaying enough social graces to show that you will fit into the work team.

This type of interview is as much about personal chemistry as anything else.

Telephone interviews

Initial screening is increasingly done via a telephone interview, particularly for jobs where communication over the telephone is important. The fundamental rules of successful telephone interviews are no different from those for other interviews, but you have to remember that your ears and voice have to do more work to compensate for the loss of visual signals. On the plus side, you can have notes of points to include and questions to ask on a table in front of you, but don't keep shuffling the papers!

If you can, avoid the following bad practice:

- 'uhms', 'ahs' and lots of false starts to sentences
- lengthy pauses where nothing seems to be happening. If you need time to think, say so.
- speaking so softly that the listener has to strain to hear you

- speaking so quickly that the listener does not grasp what you are saying, particularly if your accent is not familiar to the interviewer
- speaking in a monotone which sounds boring to the listener
- indulging in long monologues without breaks to check whether the interviewer wants to move on.

The following useful hints will help you with the etiquette of good telephone interviews.

- Listen carefully to questions and, where appropriate, paraphrase them or ask for clarification before starting to answer.
- Signal understanding or agreement with occasional interjections of 'yes' or 'mm', as nods and facial expressions are invisible.
- A smile on your face cannot be seen, but a smile in your voice can be heard. It therefore helps to smile at the other end of the phone in order to put a natural inflection into your voice.
- From time to time add phrases to check if what you are saying is adequate, relevant and not too long as you cannot see the interviewer's nods of encouragement or other controlling body language.
- Do not take it personally if the interviewer does not give much feedback on your answers. Many telephone interviews are highly structured and are designed to be fair to candidates by asking them all exactly the same questions, so that it may not feel like a normal telephone conversation. Accept that the interviewer has a job to do and may be making notes or marking a scoring chart as you speak.

One to one formal interviews

Skilful interviewers will aim to put you at your ease and you should allow them to do so, but never switch off the filter in your mind which rapidly asks. 'What is the purpose of this question?', before beginning to answer it. Nothing can really be 'off the record' in an interview, but this simply means that you have to maintain a measure of discretion over what you say, and you can still aim to be natural – 'yourself at your best' – within this setting.

The following behaviour makes it difficult for both you and the interviewer to make a success of the interview:

- a frowning or anxious facial expression
- poor eye contact
- tense or 'shrinking' posture
- monosyllabic or very brief answers
- rambling answers which upset the interviewer's schedule and make it impossible to ask all the relevant questions in the allocated timescale

- evasion of difficult issues which force the interviewer to keep probing and make the interviewee feel that the interview has turned into an inquisition
- long silences which seem like an eternity
- over-hasty answers which wind up in confusion or contradiction.

If you want to make your interviewer's day, remember the following hints:

- Always be clear about the question you are being asked to answer and seek clarification if necessary. This will help you to give more relevant answers.
- If you do not know the answer to a question, it is better to say so and allow the interviewer to move on. Do not give up too easily, however, as a moment's reflection may remind you that you can give a partial answer or a reasonable speculation based on first principles.
- Do not treat the interviewer's questions too literally if that will limit an effective response. For instance, strictly speaking, the literal answer to a question may simply be 'Yes' or 'No', but there may be an expectation that you will go on to elaborate on that answer by adding your opinion or some further information.
- Try to make the interview a pleasant experience for the interviewer by looking as if you want to be there. After all, you have to sustain conversation for half an hour, but the interviewer may face an eight hours' stint.
- If you need time to think out your answer to a complex question, ask for a few moments to draw your thoughts together. This is far better than rushing in with an ill-assorted jumble of information or half-baked ideas.
- Be well organised with questions which you want to ask, preferably relating to aspects of training and career development or the future directions of the organisation. Don't ask too many questions. By the time the interviewer gets to that stage, you are in the last few minutes of the interview.

Panel interviews

The same principles apply to panel interviews as to other types of interviews described above. The feeling of being outnumbered, however, can be over-whelming – one brain against many – and so it is as well to think through what might happen and how to conduct yourself in a panel interview.

There are a few 'don'ts' to bear in mind.

- It is very disconcerting if you always address your answers to the chair-person, irrespective of who asked the question.
- Likewise, do not maintain eye contact with only one person or, worse still, with none!
- Don't sit in a position where you cannot see all members of the panel. If necessary, ask if you can adjust the seating to gain a clear view.

Your performance will go well if you remember the following 'do's.

- You will definitely gain Brownie points if you can address individuals – correctly! – by name. This may be made easier if their names are displayed, but if not, listen carefully as they are introduced. This will also take your mind off your own initial nerves.
- Turn your attention to each questioner when giving an answer, but where appropriate include other members of the panel by quickly scanning your eyes inclusively down the line from time to time.
- If you can pick up references from previous exchanges in your answers to later questions, this shows your ability to make connections and has the effect of including the whole group in the conversation.

Other selection methods

Many organisations do not depend on interview as their sole method of selection. Some of the other selection tools which you may encounter are dealt with in this section. Further background reading on these selection methods is given in the appendix.

Psychometric tests

Many employers use aptitude, competency and personality tests to measure candidates' suitability for a particular type of work. Most of these tests are based on research on the competences and characteristics of staff who have been successful in this work. Testing should be conducted only by trained testers and feedback on their performance should be made available to those who are tested.

Some hints on psychometric tests will make them seem less daunting.

- Although practice cannot change your aptitude score from low to high, familiarity with the format of tests is helpful. Most higher education careers services hold sample materials and you may be able to arrange to do a practice test if you are eligible to use a careers service.
- Time is a key factor in aptitude tests. Do not spend precious minutes mulling over a question which you find very difficult. Press on with the next questions and come back later to the unanswered question if you have time.
- Note carefully the rules on scoring. If marks are deducted for wrong answers, it may not be safe to make inspired guesses.
- If you are likely to be severely disadvantaged because of a disability such as visual impairment, difficulty in writing or dyslexia, or if English is not your first language, bring this to the attention of the tester well in advance of the test. Designers of some tests make allowances of extra time for people in special circumstances and you may as well have the time which will enable you to give a fair representation of your ability.

- Do not try to double-guess what selectors would like you to answer in a personality test. Not only is that difficult to do, but what is the point in trying to pass yourself off as one kind of person if that is not a true picture? That would only lead to incompatibility with the job.

Presentations and lectures

If you are applying for a lecturing post, or if communication with groups or presentations of your findings is likely to be an important part of your job, it is likely that you will have to deliver a lecture or a short presentation. This may be on a topic of your choice (most likely if you are applying for an academic post) or on a theme chosen by the selectors. You may be asked to submit an outline of your talk and there may be an opportunity for the audience (which could include members of staff other than the selection panel) to ask questions.

Some careful thought in advance will avoid pitfalls.

- This exercise is about structure and delivery as well as content, so pay equal attention to all three elements.
- There is no harm in the structure being transparent. The time-honoured advice for public speaking still holds good:

    Tell them what you are going to tell them (Introduction).

    Tell them (Main content).

    Tell them what you have told them (Summary).
- Find out as much as you can in advance about who the audience will be so that you can pitch your presentation at the correct level. Will it be an audience of experts, well conversant with your field and with professional jargon, or an audience of lay people who will need a more popular version of your research findings?
- A presentation which is well structured and sound in content can be marred by ineffectual delivery. There are whole books on this subject, but the basics call for clearly audible, well-paced delivery in a voice with natural inflections which holds the interest of the audience. If you know that your voice is naturally soft, be conscious of breath control to produce greater volume. Practice with a friend in a large room where you have to project your voice for a considerable distance.
- Visual aids can be very helpful, but it requires practice to use them effectively. Remember that they also slow the pace of delivery as the audience takes in the written words, and so do not aim to have too many overhead slides if your time is very limited.
- Be sure to check what audio-visual equipment will be available. If you plan to take along your own high technology audio-visual aid, double check it before your presentation and take along an extension cable and extra batteries if these might be required.
- Practise the timing of your presentation before-hand, preferably by delivering

it to a friend or speaking it aloud into a tape recorder. Simply reading it over may give a false impression of how long it will take and you may find yourself guillotined in full flight!

Assessment centres

A variety of selection methods may be used over the space of one or two days in order to see candidates from several perspectives. This is a preferred method of larger industrial and commercial organisations, the Civil Service and some other public bodies. It is occasionally used by universities, but not usually for lecturing or research posts.

An assessment centre may consist of group discussion, group problem solving, aptitude tests, written exercises, individual and panel interviews. Most of these have been touched upon already in this chapter and there is further information in books listed in the appendix. A few hints are given below on how to cope with the extended length of the process.

- Do not try to assume a false persona to impress selectors as it will be difficult to sustain it over two or three days. Aim to be yourself, at your best.
- Try to be consistent. Apparent swings in personality between your performance in exercises and in social time will be noticed.
- Some personal space is necessary for the most gregarious person and so use any free time in the programme to reflect on the process and what you are learning from it.
- Expect to be tired after an assessment centre, and so try to get plenty of rest beforehand. If you have to come from a distance and start into the selection process on the same day, try to find the least exhausting method of travel that you or the employer can afford. Ideally, allow for a little buffer of free time between the end of your journey and the start of the assessment centre in order to have a shower, change clothes, take a walk, familiarise yourself with your surroundings, or whatever will enable you to feel on top form.
- However lavish the hospitality may be, enjoy it in moderation, and that applies to food as well as drink. The last thing you need is to be struggling with a queasy stomach or a pounding head while making a presentation or being interviewed the morning after the banquet.

Whatever interview formats or other selection methods you encounter, the main rule is to set out to enjoy them. The best generator of positive behaviour is the inner message, 'This is the stage I wanted to reach. Here is my opportunity to meet the selectors face to face and convince them that I am the right person for the job'.

Chapter 13

Developing your career strategy

Strategic planning may sound a rather grandiose phrase to apply to job seeking, but as with many activities in life, you are more likely to achieve good results if you sit down and figure out where you want to get to and what steps are involved in the journey. Random forays into the job market may occasionally succeed, but for most people it helps to have a plan.

Thinking in terms of a strategy helps you to recognise job seeking for what it is: a time-consuming occupation in which those who have planned wisely are most likely to succeed. If you think you can spare half an hour a week to organise your next move, then think again. It is much more likely to take several hours a week over an extended period of time. From the time that you see an advertisement for a job which interests you to the point at which you start work in the new job, three months can elapse, or more if you have to give a long period of notice, as is the case in many academic posts.

Your strategy is therefore a life line to help you over the long haul. If you are trying to change direction, the process is likely to take longer and may involve a period of intensive re-training. In a case like that, it is worth having both a short and a long term strategy, each of which serves a different purpose.

- Your long-term strategy helps you to keep your eyes on where you want to go. It gives you a marker against which to gauge which of the various short-term options open to you would take you in the right direction.
- Your short-term strategy keeps you conscious of the fact that you are on the move in practical ways which help you to progress. You may be doing this by filling in gaps in your experience and qualifications, by building up a network of appropriate, useful contacts, and improving both the content and the presentation of your CV.

At all times you should be clear about the relationship between your short and long term strategies. If you lose sight of this, stop and take stock before making your next move. Examples of how long and short term objectives can interconnect are given later in this chapter.

Golden rules for a job search strategy

Decide on a career before launching your job search strategy

Launching a job search strategy pre-supposes that you have made a definite decision on the career direction which you wish to pursue. If that is not the case, you may find yourself pursuing disparate goals and diffusing your energies. Not only is that a great waste of time, but it is less likely to be successful than a determined, highly focused pursuit of clear objectives.

Maximise opportunities by being flexible and open-minded

Having chosen clear objectives, it is nevertheless essential to be very flexible in how you proceed. For instance, if you look for vacancies only in the very obvious places, such as newspapers, you may well overlook numerous possibilities in the hidden job market, which is described in more detail in chapter 9.

It is too easy to limit ourselves. For instance, if you are keen to follow a particular route, is it really out of the question to undertake a period of full-time or part-time study or to work in another town? If the answer is, 'Yes', then it means that other factors in your life have a higher priority at the moment, and so the flexibility which is necessary for your strategy may have to come from considering a wider range of occupations, though these should have a recognisable coherence, in keeping with the golden rule above.

Be prepared

In the same way that you would check your equipment before commencing a research project, so it is essential to be equipped before setting out on your job search strategy. For instance, if you should be fortunate enough to meet someone who can help you on your way, you will not want to be caught short if he or she suggests that you fax through a CV immediately. Although ideally a CV should be tailored to suit each application, once you have a sense of the general direction in which you are heading, part of your short term strategy should be to have ready a good core CV which would suffice in these circumstances.

Likewise, if you know what you are looking for, in terms of either confirmation of your suitability for a post or details of vacancies, you are less likely to miss the relevance of scraps of information which would otherwise have passed you by.

Invest time and money in your job search

Many things in life have a price tag, and looking for a new job is one of them. Be realistic when assessing what these costs may be.

Some of them will be in terms of cash: a new suit for interviews; travel and overnight accommodation costs which may be incurred before they are re-imbursed; or the fees for a course of study to obtain additional qualifications.

Others may involve inroads into your time: for part-time study on top of a full-time job; using up leave for work-shadowing and other background research; customising CVs and covering letters for particular applications.

Don't set yourself impossible goals

If you set yourself a very ambitious target, don't be disappointed if you do not reach it after a single move. There may be three or four intermediate steps to take en route, but each one will be progress in the right direction.

Be realistic also about timescales. If you are unemployed and have plenty of time to give to the job search, it will still take time to implement your plan, as recruiters don't necessarily share the urgency of your agenda. If you are very busy in a current job, it can take even longer to organise your next move as it has to be fitted around other commitments.

Whatever your circumstances, it is better to keep up your morale by recording what you have achieved than to add tension by rebuking yourself for lack of speedy progress.

Take time to review and reflect

A good strategy should build in review points. In several of the case studies in chapters 7 and 8, it was when people stopped to reflect on where they were going – or not going – that they realised that they had reached a turning point at which they could see that what they had been trying to do was not working out.

Recognition that a strategy has not been working is not an acknowledgement of failure, but rather a sign of mature, analytical reflection which acts as a prelude to doing something different, which will be more effective.

Examples of short and long term strategies

The following examples demonstrate how individuals used short-term strategies to progress towards their long-term goals. Note how the people in the case studies had to remain flexible and modify their strategies to accommodate their circumstances. They had to weigh up options and assess risks, but they kept heading in the broad direction which they had chosen and did not allow themselves to be deflected from their long term goals once they had clarified what careers they wanted to pursue.

Desmond Kelly

Desmond was so caught up in the final stages of his Ph.D. in political science that he had done virtually nothing about organising employment until after submitting his thesis. On investigating options, he became interested in Civil Service competitions for the Foreign and Commonwealth Office and the European Fast Stream, leading to a placement in the European Commission. Unfortunately, he had missed the early closing dates for these competitions and so, while entry to these branches of the Civil Service remained his long-term goal, he found that he had almost a year to fill in before he could join the Civil Service. In the short term he needed some form of earnings and, ideally, an occupation which would enhance his prospects of being accepted by the Civil Service.

As a stop-gap measure, Desmond kept on his part-time job as a tutorial assistant in his department, thinking that this would stand him in good stead if he decided on an academic career in future. He supplemented his modest income with a few shifts in a European call centre for a bank in order to maintain and improve his language skills and demonstrate his customer service orientation.

At his Careers Service he found out about the European Commission's six month 'stages', or placements in Directorates in Brussels, Luxembourg or Strasbourg. This would give him a good insight into the Commission's affairs while giving him access to first-class language tuition. It would also help Desmond to decide whether a career in administration would suit him. Whether or not he subsequently entered the Civil Service, a 'stage' would enhance his CV and greatly increase his employability in the eyes of many recruiters.

Desmond was advised to lobby his Euro-MP to support his application for a 'stage'. After doing so, he was offered temporary employment as a research assistant in the Euro-MP's constituency office, an opportunity which he seized and which greatly assisted his selection as a 'stagiaire'. Although he enjoyed being a Parliamentary researcher, Desmond's sights are still set on eventual entry to the Foreign and Commonwealth Office as it offers greater security and better promotion prospects in the long term.

Margaret Osmond

Following a first class honours degree and a Master's degree in psychology, Margaret was employed as a research assistant in the department from which she had graduated. Her research was on the influence of peers in health education programmes and it brought her into contact with health educators and other paramedical workers.

After eighteen months on this project, Margaret applied for a doctoral programme in clinical psychology and was very disappointed to be rejected. Thinking that her academic track record and recent work experience should have made her an ideal candidate, she sought feedback from the selectors to see how she could improve an application for the following year. Their advice was that they were looking for a more practical kind of health-related experience, possibly including contact with patients, in addition to all that Margaret had to offer.

This feedback put Margaret in a dilemma. If she were to leave academic work, would she be closing that door behind her without knowing if the door to clinical psychology would open the next time that she knocked on it? Being in a quandary, Margaret sought advice from academic colleagues and formed the opinion that a short period of work in a related practical field could be shown to advantage in her CV should she decide to apply for academic jobs in the future. She knew, however, that three or four years away from academia without publication could be detrimental to her return.

Deciding to take the risk, Margaret took up a post as a support worker in a voluntary organisation dealing with patients recovering from head injuries. As the pay in this job was low, she supplemented her income by offering tuition to 'A' level and undergraduate students, knowing that this would also stand her in good stead should she wish to apply later for an academic post. As it happened, however, she was accepted for a clinical psychology course at the next intake, having used her supervisor at the head injuries rehabilitation centre as one of her referees.

Working out your strategy

The above examples show how two people developed their career plans by co-ordinating their short and long-term job search strategies. You can use the rest of this chapter to help you to begin to think through your own strategic plan. This will not – and cannot – be written in tablets of stone. You cannot predict the opportunities which will come your way or the constraints which may curb your freedom of action. Nonetheless, if you work out a broad career direction in which you intend to move, you are much more likely to arrive at a satisfactory destination than if you drift through life aimlessly.

The framework outlined below will help you to follow through a logical process of thought and action if you have by now chosen a long term career goal, even though that may be fairly broad at this stage. If you are still having difficulty in homing in on a specific group of occupations (e.g. the media or public sector regulatory bodies), read again chapters 2 to 4 which deal with self-assessment and the process of matching yourself against suitable occupations. You may also find it helpful to discuss your fragmentary ideas with a professional careers adviser who can help you to identify patterns and themes which will point to certain career preferences. You can then return to this chapter to move on towards action planning.

When you are ready to start devising the strategy which will help you to progress towards your long term career goal, the following framework will help you to structure your thinking in a logical sequence.

- What are your preferred career options?
- What will you need to have in place before you can move in this direction?
- What can you offer at the moment?
- What do you still need to achieve?
- What are all the possible routes you could take?
- Weigh up the advantages and disadvantages of these various routes by thinking about obstacles which may make some routes less desirable than others.
- Based on this thinking, what do you think are your preferred routes?

- Once you have chosen preferred routes, which people or factors can help you to make progress?
- What timescale will you attach to your plan in order to keep moving forward?

The next section of the book helps you to see what is involved in working through each of these stages and gives you examples based on Desmond and Margaret.

Your preferred career options

At this stage you can state either a specific job title or a broad career direction. The more specific you can be, the easier it will be to handle the next stages of the planning process. You may, of course, have more than one career goal in mind. For instance, Margaret still had one eye on an academic research career while gathering experience for entry to clinical psychology. If you are considering several options, you can repeat the process described in Exercise 13.1 for various occupations.

Essential and desirable requirements

Here you need to face the facts about what it will take to gain entry to your preferred career options. If you are not sure how to gather information about careers, refer to chapter 5 which gives you some starting points.

Do not be daunted when you realise all that is required for you to reach your goal. It is important to realise what is involved (Exercise 13.2). If you are really interested in a particular career, you should regard the pre-requisites for entry not as barriers designed to exclude you, but as landmarks, the achievement of which will let you know that you are still headed in the right direction. Had Desmond and Margaret been deflected at the first hurdle, their ambitions would never have been achieved.

Exercise 13.1 Selecting preferred career options

	Preferred option
Desmond	An intellectually stimulating occupation involving international contemporary affairs in the public sector.
Margaret	Clinical psychology
Myself	

Exercise 13.2 Entry requirements

Career	What is required for entry
International public affairs	*Essential*
	Evidence of interest in international current affairs High intellectual ability Good interpersonal skills, including tact and diplomacy Highly developed communication skills Flexibility and mobility
	Highly desirable
	A relevant honours degree Fluency in foreign languages Knowledge of international institutions
Clinical psychology	*Essential*
	A good honours degree in psychology Practical experience of working with patients or people with psychological difficulties Good interpersonal skills An ability to remain professionally objective
	Highly desirable
	Training in research methods
My own option	*Essential*
	Highly desirable

Summary of what you can offer

This is where you describe the point from which you are starting out. You are certainly not starting out with a blank page. Use the work which you did in chapter 3 on your skills, interests, values and temperament. You will also be able to add your qualifications and directly relevant or transferable work and life experience.

The difference between what you assembled in chapter 3 and what you are doing

now is that in the earlier exercises you drew on everything which had a bearing on
your self-assessment. Now that you are being more specific about your options, you
will select those aspects which are relevant to that career, in the way that was
explained in chapter 10 when looking at the selection of facts for inclusion in a CV.

The table in Exercise 13.3 summarises where Desmond and Margaret started
out from as they began to implement their strategic plan. Add your own position
at present.

Exercise 13.3 Matching entry requirements

	What can I offer
Desmond	*Essential requirements*
	Good knowledge of international current affairs through political research, the media, membership of student political and debating societies Ph.D. degree gives evidence of intellectual ability Personal skills developed through summer jobs and leisure activities
	Highly desirable requirements
	Degrees in political science Somewhat rusty school level French Basic theoretical knowledge of international institutions
Margaret	*Essential requirements*
	Two good degrees in psychology Some contact with health educators and paramedics and observation of interviews with their clients Evidence of personal skills from non-relevant summer jobs and interaction with professionals during her research Objectivity needed in research, but not tested in potentially emotive situations
	Highly desirable requirements
	Good knowledge of research methods through degrees
Myself	*Essential requirements*
	Highly desirable requirements

Targets for achievement

When you subtract what you can already offer from the total of what you need to achieve in order to succeed, you can see clearly what you still have to put in place. These targets become your short term goals, or the landmarks along your route to success.

You also have to bring a measure of realism into this stage of your planning. If, for instance, Desmond had decided that for personal reasons he could not be mobile or that he had a severe weakness in learning foreign languages, he might well have reviewed his specific objectives and branched out in a different direction.

In Exercise 13.4, quantify what remains to be achieved, just as Desmond and Margaret did at the beginning of their strategic planning.

Exercise 13.4 Targets for achievement

Desmond	*Essential requirements*
	Closer acquaintance with international affairs at a more practical level, ideally, from within an international governmental organisation
	Further development of personal skills in a relevant work setting, supported by a good reference from an employer
	Highly desirable requirements
	Improve fluency of French
	Begin learning another language
	Gain first hand knowledge of an international public body
Margaret	*Essential requirements*
	Practical work experience in a medical or voluntary sector setting
	Evidence of personal skills in relation to people with psychological difficulties
	Evidence of professional objectivity in a practical rather than a purely theoretical setting
Myself	*Essential requirements*
	Highly desirable requirements

Choosing routes to develop your plan

Having assessed what needs to be done, you may find that there is only one way to proceed. For instance, Margaret could not qualify as a clinical psychologist without taking a relevant postgraduate qualification. In many cases, however, there may be several options which could lead in a similar direction and individuals may be suited by one route rather than another. For example, there were numerous options open to Margaret while she was acquiring the experience necessary before beginning the clinical psychology course.

Use Exercise 13.5 (page 179) to review the range of possibilities open to you in your short-term strategy. If you feel that you may not know of all the options, discuss them with a careers adviser or a practitioner in the field which you hope to enter.

Helping hands

There is a tremendous amount of untapped good will in the world. For example, if you had information which would help someone on his or her way to career success, you would most probably share it. It therefore pays to ask for help and advice. If people do not know that you are on the move, they cannot help you.

Table 13.1 Desmond's options

Options	Considerations	Ranking
'Stage' in the European Commission	Six months' time lag before entry - but worth proceeding Highly competitive – but lobbying Euro-MP is known to help	1
Temporary jobs	Necessary for income – therefore high priority Choose so as to be able to show relevance to future plans: e.g. tutoring in Political Science developing language and customer service skills	1
Further postgraduate study: – international relations – foreign languages	Very attractive, but not practical in terms of finance Already have two degrees – what is lacking is work experience	3
Other language tuition	Could brush up on French through private study – may lose motivation Could pay a foreign language student a small sum for conversation classes – sounds more interesting	2

Table 13.2 Margaret's options

Options	Considerations	Ranking
Research assistant and part-time voluntary work	Best option financially, but may not acquire enough practical experience for entry to clinical psychology	2
Full-time work with patients	Quicker way to gain necessary experience, but income insufficient for commitments	1
Tutorial assistant (20hrs)	Good option for possible career in academia, but preparation and marking very time consuming	3
Private tuition (6 hrs)	Less time-consuming, but still keeps link with academia	1

Exercise 13.5 My short-term options

Option	Considerations	Ranking

Timescale for action

Both Desmond and Margaret had definite timescales imposed by closing dates for the type of work or course they wished to enter, but as these dates were far ahead, they had to organise the intervening months in order to have everything in place by the time they applied for the next stage (Tables 13.5 and 13.6).

Your career objectives may not have such definite timescales, but to avoid drifting with no sense of urgency or bolting prematurely into ill-prepared actions, it is as well to give yourself some realistic target dates in order to ensure that you keep up the momentum (Exercise 13.7, page 181).

Table 13.3 Desmond's network

Areas of interest	Potential helpers
European commission 'stage'	Careers adviser Euro information office Euro-MP

Table 13.4 Margaret's network

Areas of interest	Potential helpers
Appropriate work experience for clinical psychology	Clinical psychologist practitioner Clinical psychology course tutor Health educators and paramedics Local Volunteer Bureau Own GP

Exercise 13.6 My network

Areas of interest	Potential helpers

Table 13.5 Desmond's timetable

Date	Action
October	Extension of part-time contract as a tutorial assistant Apply for part-time job
November	Begin call centre job with spell of intensive customer service training
January	Commence evening class in French Investigate European Commission 'stage' option Send for 'stage' application materials
February	Consult Careers Service on quality of application
March	Contact Euro-MP for support with application
April	Offered temporary employment with Euro-MP Reduced call centre hours to accommodate new job Send off 'stage' application with Euro-MP as referee
August	Apply for Foreign and Commonwealth Office for the following year
September	Commence stagiaire post

Table 13.6 Margaret's timetable

Date	Action
July	Seek advice from selectors on how to enhance application for clinical psychology
August	Investigation of appropriate options in voluntary sector – including visits to projects
September	Applications, including one to Head Injuries Trust. References sought by employers
October	Interview and appointment as a project worker
November	Re-application for clinical psychology course Begin tutoring A level and undergraduate students to supplement income
January	Take advantage of in-service training course for support workers
February	Interview for clinical psychology course
April	Notification of acceptance for clinical psychology course Begin to apply for funding for course

Exercise 13.7 My timetable

Date	Action

Summary

You should now have a better understanding of the entire process of career choice, from self-assessment and the gathering of occupational information, through decision making and on to the self-presentation skills which will assist you in selection procedures. You know that strategic planning can assist your movement through the whole process and can see how short term strategies are designed to help you to achieve all the pre-requisites for entry to your chosen field, while long term strategies help you to keep focusing on your career objective, even if these seem to be set a fair distance ahead of you.

Understanding the process, knowing where to turn for help and having a timetable for action should help you to feel that you will ultimately succeed. You may find that your career develops in ways which are not identical to your original objective because in the process you may have seized opportunities which you could not have foreseen or re-focused your aims as your knowledge of the total range of options grew. That really does not matter as long as you feel that the general direction in which you have travelled is compatible with where you want to be.

The case studies throughout this book demonstrate that numerous people who have set out from where you are now have built successful careers which have given them job satisfaction. If you believe in your own capabilities and are willing to combine realism with determination, success is within your grasp. Aim high if that is what you wish, but above all aim for self-fulfilment in a career which stimulates your interest and brings you rewards which have meaning and value for you.

Sources of information

Career choice

Hopson, Barrie (1984), *Build Your Own Rainbow: a workbook for career and life management*, Lifeskills.
Bolles, Richard Nelson, (1997) *What Colour is Your Parachute?*, Ten Speed Press, Berkeley.
PROSPECTS (HE) computer aided guidance system. Available in many higher education careers services and sometimes networked across campuses.

Occupational information

PROSPECTS (HE) Website - http://www.prospects.csu.ac.uk.
AGCAS information booklets, Central Services Unit (CSU), Manchester. Available in higher education careers services or for purchase from CSU at Prospect House, Booth Street East, Manchester, M13 9EP.
Occupations 1999, COIC, Thames Ditton.
British Qualifications (29th edition) (1998), Kogan Page, London.
Training Access Point. Careers database available in some local careers company offices, libraries, Jobcentres, colleges and universities.

Employer information

PROSPECTS (HE) Website - http://www.prospects.csu.ac.uk.
PROSPECTS Directory, CSU (annually), Manchester.
CRAC, *Graduate Employment and Training* (annual), Hobsons Publishing, Cambridge
Corporate Research Foundation UK (1997), *Britain's Best Employers* (1997), McGraw-Hill, Maidenhead.
UK: Kompass Register (annual), Reed Information Services, East Grinstead. Also available for 46 countries worldwide.
Internet websites of individual employers and higher education institutions.
Regional directories of Training and Enterprise Councils (England and Wales) and Local Enterprise Companies (Scotland).

Vacancy information

AGCAS Scotland – SGCP (1998 revised edition), *Guide to Job Search via the Internet for Academic Researchers*. Covers sources of academic and non-academic vacancies. Available from the Robert Gordon University Careers Service, Schoolhill, Aberdeen

The Times Higher Education Supplement (weekly, Fridays).

Willing's Press Guide (annually). A guide to the press of the United Kingdom and to the principal publications of Europe, USA and the Gulf States: for details of publications relevant to particular professions.

Selection process

AGCAS information booklets, *Job Seeking Strategies*, *Making Applications*, *Going for Interviews*, available from CSU, Prospects House, Booth Street East, Manchester, M13 9EP.

AGCAS videos, *Looking Good on Paper*, *Why Ask Me That?*, *Two Whole Days*, available in higher education careers services.

AGCAS Scotland – SGCP, *Managing Your Career*, self-help resource pack (see section one).

Phillips, C., (1996), *First Interviews – Sorted!*, GTI, St Albans.

Yate, M. J., (1995), *Great Answers to Tough Interview Questions*, Kogan Page, London.

Notes

Chapter 1

1 *Realising Their Potential: Report of the Contract Research Staff Initiative*, Scottish Higher Education Funding Council (SHEFC), 1997, p. 8.
2 Figures provided by the Scottish Higher Education Funding Council, based on data collected by the Higher Education Statistics Agency (see Table 1.2).
3 K. Mackenzie, *Destinations of Contract Research Staff in some Scottish Universities: a Pilot Study*, Scottish Graduate Careers Partnership, Glasgow, 1997.
4 *Good Employment Practice: University Contract Researchers*, Association of University Teachers, 1991.
5 *Commitment Betrayed: a Survey of Contract Research Staff in UK Universities*, Association of University Teachers, 1994.
6 *Realising our Potential: a Strategy for Science, Engineering and Technology*, HMSO, 1993.
7 *Academic Research Careers for Graduate Scientists*, House of Lords Select Committee on Science and Technology, HMSO, 1995.
8 Published September 1996, available from the Committee of Vice-Chancellors and Principals.
9 The main research councils are: The Biotechnology and Biological Sciences Research Council, the Engineering and Physical Sciences Research Council, the Economic and Social Sciences Research Council, the Medical Research Council, the Natural Environment Research Council and the Particle Physics and Astronomy Research Council. The three main bodies are: The Committee of Vice-Chancellors and Principals, the Standing Conference of Principals, the Committee of Scottish Higher Education Principals.
10 *Concordat on Contract Research Staff Career Management*, CVCP circular, 1/97/26, May 1997.
11 *Realising Their Potential: Report of the Contract Research Staff Initiative*, SHEFC, 1997.
12 Commitment Betrayed: a Survey of Contract Research Staff in UK Universities, Association of University Teachers, 1994.

Chapter 2

1 A. G. Watts, 'Careers Education in Higher Education: Principles and Practice' *British Journal of Guidance and Counselling*, vol. 5, no. 2, 1977.

Chapter 3

1 List from 'Where Next' resource pack, Association of Graduate Careers Advisory Services.

Chapter 7

1 The Teaching Company Scheme promotes partnerships between companies and universities, employing graduates to work on technical or commercial projects for the company on a two-year contract. Most Teaching Company Associates simultaneously register for a higher degree.

2 G. Reiss, *Project Management Demystified*, E. and F. N. Spon, London, 1992, p. 21.

Index